SISTERCELEBRATIONS

Nine Worship Experiences

edited by

ARLENE SWIDLER

FORTRESS PRESS   Philadelphia

BV
4844
.S97
1974

hit
76
Sw63

Biblical quotations from the Revised Standard Version of the
Bible, copyrighted 1946 and 1952 by the Division of Christian
Education of the National Council of the Churches of Christ in
the United States of America, are used by permission.

Library of Congress Catalog Card Number 74-80414

ISBN 0-8006-1084-9

4263D74   Printed in U.S.A.   1-1084

CONTENTS

CONTRIBUTORS

Carol Adams, who has been a Rockefeller fellow at Yale Divinity School, is an intern for women at the University of Pennsylvania Christian Association; she has a special interest in women's history.

Ellen Charry, a graduate of Barnard College and Yeshiva University's School of Social Work, is currently working in Jewish education with a special interest in creative approaches to prayer. Dana Charry is a psychiatrist with a broad background in Jewish studies; before studying medicine, he spent a number of years as a religious teacher and Jewish youth leader.

C. Virginia Finn, who has a master's degree in Speech, is the mother of six young children and a part-time speech instructor in Milwaukee; she has edited the *Bulletin* of the U.S. Section of St. Joan's Alliance since 1970.

Clare Benedicks Fischer, now completing her Ph.D. in the Sociology of Religion at the Graduate Theological Union in Berkeley, California, is on the staff of the Office of Women's Affairs there.

Sydney H. Pendleton, a nurse who has acted as consultant to the Pan American Health Organization, is finishing a doctorate in nursing research with a concentration in anthropology.

Gail Anderson Ricciuti, an ordained minister of the United Presbyterian Church, is currently assistant pastor of the Central Presbyterian Church in Massillon, Ohio.

Maurine Stephens, a graduate of Union Theological Seminary in New York City, is now Co-Minister of the Christian Association at the University of Pennsylvania; she wrote an M.Div. thesis on the ethics of abortion.

Aviva Cantor Zuckoff, a graduate of Barnard College and the Columbia University School of Journalism, has been assistant American bureau chief of the *London Jewish Chronicle*, editor of the Socialist-Zionist *Jewish Liberation Journal*, and a founding staff member of *Lilith Magazine*.

PREFACE

For the past two or three years, while the mass media have been concentrating on the women fighting for equal pay and job opportunities, other women have been at work rethinking their whole identity as daughters of God. Sometimes alone, more often together, they have looked at their churches and synagogues with a new feminist eye, seen a lot of weaknesses they had never noticed before, and then gone on to try to present to their faith communities a vision of the way things can be in the future.

These liturgies are the result of such efforts. They represent women's answers to a lot of new questions: What does the Bible tell me about my freedom as a daughter of God? How do I see my womanhood as a reflection of God? Who are the women that I myself want to imitate? How do I as a woman experience sin? What does it mean to be a woman?

Some of the liturgies come from ecumenical groups of women, others are more specific—Jewish, Roman Catholic, Episcopal. One was written by a university religion class; several come from college campuses; others were designed within parishes. But some of the same emphases occur in almost all of these services: a respect for tradition combined with the courage to use it in new ways, a care that the entire congregation can participate actively in the worship, a search for new symbols, a constant feeling that these liturgies are not finished products but just steps along an unending path.

The liturgies make good reading; many of them had already been passing from hand to hand in mimeographed form before this book took shape. The writers hoped that other women—and men—would want to try their hands at expressing feminist values too.

But all of our writers are concerned that other groups do their own thing—that other religion classes think through all the theological implications of women's liberation and express them in their own way; that other women's groups take the time to reassess their personal and communal goals for themselves. "This shouldn't be a collection of services from which women just choose something to replay for their own group," they kept telling us. "What we are putting together should be an idea-book, a mind-opener."

So what we have done is to ask each of these liturgy-designers to write a very personal essay about the whole liturgical process—to tell us just how the idea for the liturgy arose, what the writers were trying to do in the liturgy, what kinds of problems they faced, how the whole thing worked out in action, how both they and the congregation felt about the experience.

The sample liturgies and the introductions with their practical advice will add up, we think, to a handbook for women who want to begin creating their own liturgies for meetings, conventions, holidays, commencements, Sunday mornings, installations of officers—or any other occasion.

Arlene Swidler

GOD OF THE MATRIARCHS

Gail Anderson Ricciuti

The last autumn I spent at Princeton Theological Seminary in Princeton, New Jersey, the mood between the men and women on campus was generally one of tension and hostility. A group of women seminarians of which I was a member had been made extremely sensitive to the issues of the women's liberation movement by the invariably sarcastic and condescending treatment of all too many clergy and laymen. Prompted by these sensitivities, we sponsored a fall speaking appearance on our campus by a leading militant feminist. Her confrontation with the students, both male and female, fulfilled one hope of our group—to bring out in the open our struggle for recognition as full and responsible human beings. Instead of fostering a new understanding of these issues among the students, however, her words and manner (whether justifiable or not) proved abrasive—contributing further to the alienation already prevailing on campus. It was in this atmosphere that I began to prepare for a weekday chapel service I was to lead for the seminary community.

One morning during this daily worship, as I pondered a theme for my service, I was jolted by the words of a vocal selection being sung by a male seminarian, in which he addressed the "God of Abraham, Isaac, and Jacob." I had heard the words often before, but this time they startled me like someone rattling the bars of a prison door; and immediately there popped into my thoughts, almost like a protest: "God of Sarah, Rebekah, and Rachel!" From that seed grew this liturgy, "God of the Matriarchs."

It struck me not only that the models of righteousness in our prayers are usually men, but that even the models of sinfulness are male! We pervert the Christian faith by denying women even their identity as *sinners*! And it seemed to me that if one were to construct a "model" liturgy which could lead women and men alike before God as creatures of his making, then one would have to have the integrity to picture *both* as sinful, as well as possessing the potential for redemption and renewal. It was easy to find in the Bible models of "fallen" women for the responsive Prayer of Confession; but the difficulty I encountered (which was perhaps to be expected, given the bias of the times in which Scripture took form) was that of finding women as well as men to use as models of faithfulness and righteousness for the Litany of Praise and Hope.

The Litany was intended to do three things: to provide a context of growth and empathy by requiring the men to give thanks for the lives of great women and the women to give thanks for outstanding men (many of us found these words difficult to pray!) and to strengthen the self-image of both groups by allowing them to identify with solid models of their own sex. Finally, the rhythm of male and female voices alternating in the address and then joining in the petitions was planned deliberately as an avenue of symbolic reconciliation.

In spite of my own bitter feelings over my treatment by male colleagues, I resolved not to use my position of "power" as worship leader of a captive audience to "retaliate" with more direct confrontation—which was tempting to do. Rather, by trying to construct a worship service in which both women and men could participate with sincerity and integrity, I hoped to provide a climate in which what was *not* said could bring about more healing than what *could have been* said. I cannot honestly pretend that I was optimistic about how this type of liturgy would be received. But I approached the service as a statement I felt had to be made at the time, whatever the consequences.

With that in mind, the response to the liturgy on the morning it was presented was astounding! The spirit which grew in the congregation of students and faculty as we shared these prayers, and as I spoke informally and nonjudgmentally of some of my own feelings and struggles as a woman, was a beautiful, healing experience. This type of approach somehow provided the catharsis needed to resolve much of the resentment which had been smoldering among us.

I have used this particular liturgy only one other time, at a clinic for pastors' wives led by my husband Anthony (who is himself a Presbyterian minister); and on this occasion too it met with an enthusiastic response from many women who feel themselves "sidelined" in the mission of the church. The Prayer of Confession and the Litany have also been used effectively at least twice.

On the basis of this experience, I would suggest to designers of feminist liturgies that a litany such as this will be effective and remembered if it is presented not to judge or accuse but in a spirit of acceptance. Our aim should be to minister to the needs of all who participate in the service, and to offer them new alternatives for worship as well as a new self-image before God. The fact that the means and mode of worship both *presuppose* a certain self-image and *build* a self-image might be the most important thing to keep in mind in setting out to write prayers. I feel it was this quality of upholding the personhood of *both* male and female rather than elevating one at the expense of the other that might hold out the best hope for needed reform in Christian worship.

GOD OF THE MATRIARCHS

"I sent Moses to lead you, with . . . Miriam."

PRELUDE

CALL TO WORSHIP

HYMN: "O God, Thou Art the Father"

PRAYER OF CONFESSION

Leader: If we claim to be sinless, we are self-deceived and strangers to the truth . . . and then his word has no place in us.

All: Hear us, O God, as we recall those who have sinned before us and, admitting ourselves to be in their lineage, attempt to become truthful before you.

* * * * *(silence)*

Leader: "But I have this against you, that you tolerate the woman Jezebel, who calls herself a prophetess and is teaching and beguiling my servants to practice immorality and to eat food sacrificed to idols." (*Rev. 2:20*)

All: We confess our forgetfulness, Lord, that you alone are God. We have followed after Jezebel, shameless lover of idols, worshiping other gods, exalting ourselves and our own dogmas at each other's expense. O God, claim our hearts once more.

* * * *

Leader: "When Delilah saw that (Samson) had told her all his mind, she sent and called the lords of the Philistines, saying, 'Come up this once, for he has told me all his mind.' Then the lords of the Philistines came up to her, and brought the money in their hands. . . . Then she began to torment him, and his strength left him." (*Judg. 16:18, 19*)

All: We confess that we are often offspring of Delilah: eager to learn the secrets of others, we misuse our knowledge and bring them to ruin. God of truth, teach us to respect the truth.

* * * *

Leader: "The sun had risen on the earth when Lot came to Zoar. Then the Lord rained on Sodom and Gomorrah brimstone and fire from the Lord out of heaven. . . . But Lot's wife behind him looked back, and she became a pillar of salt." (*Gen. 19:23–24, 25*)

All: God of justice and mercy, we would not perish like the wife of Lot in our nearsighted clinging to the old and familiar. But we are woefully lacking in singleness of heart. Challenge us again.

* * * *

Leader: "The scribes and the Pharisees brought a woman who had been caught in the act of adultery, and . . . they said to him, 'Teacher . . . in the law Moses commanded us to stone such. What do you say about her?' . . . But when they heard it, they went away, one by one . . . and Jesus said, 'Neither do I condemn you; go, and do not sin again.' " (*John 8:3, 4, 9, 11*)

All: Like that woman, may we, too, be surprised by the discovery of our true selves—new selves—in the light of your grace! Do not forget us, Lord; but lead us always nearer our heritage as your daughters and sons. In the name of Jesus Christ, let it be!

ASSURANCE OF PARDON

SCRIPTURE: Luke 1:26–55

HYMN: "Lo, How a Rose E'er Blooming"

MEDITATION

I have found Mary, the mother of Jesus, to be a paradigm of many of the feelings I have shared with other women who also feel themselves called to some special service in the church. We are told that Mary was deeply troubled over this strange new role when the angel appeared to her; and after he announced that she was to be the bearer of the Word, the Savior, the One who was to come to the throne of David, Mary asked the angel, "How can this be . . .?" His answer was that this was the work of the Holy Spirit, and "with God *nothing* will be impossible." Henceforth Mary saw herself in a new way: "Behold, I *am* the handmaid of the Lord." It was a word of acceptance of the challenge and calling.

We have also the eloquent song of Mary, the Magnificat, exclaiming in delight and affirmation, "He has regarded the low estate of his handmaiden." For in a world in which women were not even numbered among the human souls required to constitute a synagogue, in which women still counted as possessions of men, it was Mary—a woman—who was called to bear the Word. How little things have changed in two thousand years! Early in her calling, Mary recognized that God does indeed put down the mighty from their thrones and exalt those of low degree.

Even at the time for her delivery, when the Word was to be revealed, Mary was turned away from the inn which should have received her. Nevertheless, she *did* give birth: the Word could not be turned aside or foiled, once it was spoken by God.

And so it is, from beginning to beginning, that women were favored first with the message of salvation. Mary was chosen to bear him figuratively—bodily; the women at the tomb bore the news verbally. They were commissioned, as we are no less than our husbands or male counterparts, to go quickly and tell: not primarily to arrange flowers or wash communion glasses, but in a multitude of creative and challenging ways, to enter the whole work of ministry!

So there is hope for us. In spite of prejudice and hesitancy within the church, I cannot believe that the One who called us, be we women or men, will frustrate his purpose. Perhaps some future generation will call *us* blessed because we too were called to bear the Word. In the words of her kinswoman Elizabeth, as her own unborn child leaped for joy at the sound of Mary's voice, "Blessed is she who believed that there would be a fulfillment of what was spoken to her from the Lord!"

LITANY OF PRAISE AND HOPE

Leader: Let us not falter in hope! Let us offer our praise and our lives to the Lord.

Men: God of the patriarchs. . .

Women: God of the matriarchs. . .

All: In line with all your faithful people in every age, we offer again ourselves and our gifts for the service of your kingdom!

Women: God of Abraham, Isaac, and Jacob. . .

Men: God of Sarah, Rebekah, and Rachel. . .

All: Grant us the courage to cling to your promise, even if all the world seems hostile and our own hearts judge us failures.

Men: God of Priscilla and Aquilla. . .

Women: God of Moses and of Miriam. . .

All: May we too labor in harmony to bring our people out of bondage and darkness.

Women: O God of Deborah, a mother in Israel, greatest of Israel's judges. . .

Men: O God of Solomon, the wisest of kings. . .

All: May our lives be but mirrors of your justice, lived out in the wisdom of unswerving faith.

Women: Great God of Lydia, seller of purple. . .

Men: Master of Paul, a maker of tents. . .

All: Guide us into the world unafraid to lend our hands as well as our voices to your service, and eager to involve ourselves with all of your children.

Men: And for the lives of all righteous women. . .

Women: For past and present men of faith. . .

All: For the ministries taking form within us, and for all the callings yet to be: The Lord's Name be Praised!

BENEDICTION

POSTLUDE

THE, LORD'S NAME, BE PRAIS ED

SANDY BAUER '74

2

MOTHERHOOD REBORN

Clare Benedicks Fischer

Most of the women enrolled for our spring course in "Women and Theology" at the Graduate Theological Union had also participated in the corresponding classes convened the previous fall and winter. They had helped give shape to the class and were quite prepared for a "workshop" approach to the subject matter. In addition to the weekly evening lectures, which were structured around the growth of American feminism and its connection with religion and church history, there were afternoon sessions involving an experimental use of our personal selves and the more formal data of the course. Such a workshop was, at first, easier to plan than to implement.

The first couple of sessions were, in retrospect, a curious blend of the "rap" group process, in which we shared our experiences, and a mutual sharing of how we would encounter the frustrations and difficulties of the practical world of denominations, churches, and jobs. On one occasion we enacted a socio-drama, working out situations involving stereotypes and hurtful remarks. This session helped to create a trusting and informal atmosphere—which probably had something to do with the receptivity the group evidenced when I suggested, the following week, that we plan a liturgy.

The invitation to do a liturgy had a remarkable effect on the class. Although we were consciously attempting to construct a community among ourselves, and sensed that the class was an exception to the traditional academic exchange, we had not really experienced a "coming together." Like the proverbial "flash," the idea of creating and presenting a liturgy transformed all the participants: we sensed that we could accomplish an important "something" and actually have fun in the process! The workshop suddenly ceased to be a problematic experience; it became instead a pleasurable engagement which provided the opportunity to explore and share our skills. We had spoken about woman's place in society, and how she is intimidated when she has to be a "public self," but now we could put into practice our deep conviction that women can be audible in a creative and meaningful setting. The enthusiasm to get on with the planning was gratifying!

The workshop became a weekly session of organizing tasks, testing ideas, and intensive exchanges—all leading up to the presentation of two liturgies: one for the students and faculty of the Graduate Theological Union community during the regular chapel hour; the other, to be held on Mother's Day, a slightly expanded version for the larger community. The theme, "Motherhood Reborn," had been collectively chosen at the first planning session, after much discussion about maternity and its connection with divinity. One member of the group had been at the interfaith summer conference at Grailville, Ohio, where women had sought an approach to "feminine theology"; Karen suggested that we improvise on the four motifs of grounding, creating, nuturing, and liberating. "Liberating" was then changed to express the "mothering" notion of "delivery."

These motifs helped us to organize and structure the liturgy and clearly indicated our affirming mood. We shared a festive spirit—in our ability to collaborate

and create with ease and in the message of joy we had
to tell. But we grappled with a way to celebrate through
images as well as words and realized that both the
dramatic and the participatory had to be integral
aspects of our "celebration." For song and music we
recruited two talented women singers who were not
students at GTU but were involved in the seminary
community. They planned with us and helped us to
experience the reality that community *is* in the sharing,
not in the perfunctory belonging. A dance liturgy class
provided the opportunity for a cooperative project
between men and women students, and our dancers
brought to life—through motion—a dimensionality of
our notion of nurturing and the feminine which had not
surfaced through words alone. We decided that our
liturgy had to end with involvement beyond ourselves,
and together we recognized that an "open litany" of
testimonials might produce such participation. Being a
little uncertain about whether the congregation would
enter into this activity, each of us had something in
mind to say at the appropriate time. However, we had
no reason to fear: many spontaneous responses closed
the distance between the liturgists and the congregation.

The congeniality of the planning process was not
unmarked by controversy. Although the selection of
readings from the Old and New Testaments was something of a happening, each of us paging through the
Bible and reading aloud various passages, we were able
to settle upon the particular readings agreeably. Our
controversy was sparked by the question of translation
and the reading of the pronoun "he" or "she." Now we
saw how the abstract issue of who our God is had to
give way to an authentic understanding of an andro-
gynous, or perhaps sexless, Godhead. After several
heated exchanges, where a serious listening to one

another emerged from the first impatient quibblings about words, we were able to arrive at a strong and united position. We had theologized together and come to a view which allowed us to proclaim the feminine pronoun—without intimidation or discomfort—as a concrete *sign* of the feminine "motifs."

Our presentation to the GTU community was to be compacted into a forty-minute experience, while our Sunday presentation allowed for improvisation and refinement. On both occasions we wanted the personal reflections of women—and the praise of specific women who helped us realize our strengths—to be as central as the reading from sacred text and song and dance. Ann had shared with us at various times her pleasure in motherhood as a fact, and she offered to express this to the whole liturgical community. Karen had been our resource person for the notion of the "motifs," and she amiably agreed to contribute a theological statement. A subcommittee of the class had worked out the Credal Statement, the Open Litany, and the Corporate Responses. Without "dress rehearsals" but with a good deal of anticipation we came together on the two particular occasions as a community with a message; we offered our celebration as a "confident gift."

Our publicity for the Tuesday chapel presentation at GTU was minimal. In addition to announcing it in the Pacific School of Religion bulletin we circulated a flier and told our friends. The turnout was larger than usual, and gave us a strong sense that what we were about was important. Our pacing of the liturgy was perfect. We combined voice and silence, placement and movement in a dramatic manner. On this first occasion no one spoke from the center-front except the woman who called the congregation to worship. On the spur of the moment we decided to locate ourselves at random throughout the chapel. In this way we hoped to dispel both the separating notion of "being in front" and the cluster-look. There was something very exciting in having the participants rise from unexpected places around the church. I believe that this random distribution encouraged others to join in the Open Litany. After we had left the chapel, singing and holding hands, we were greeted with excited and happy exclamations and embraces. Those who had come had indeed experienced our message.

We were heady with success. However, we had yet to complete our preparations for the second liturgy. We decided to provide a longer litany on Sunday and have something "symbolic" occur. We jokingly talked about giving everyone a seed, and then planting the seeds after the celebration. That idea developed into the one which was actually used: the planting of a tiny tree which would be left in the sanctuary as our gift. I offered to have my daughter enact this with me (after I had consulted with her about her participation in the tree planting as well as in the reading of a poem).

Our second presentation was clearly more polished, and that may not have been advantageous. On Sunday the dancers were not available, and despite several press releases about the liturgy there were considerably fewer people than on Tuesday. I suspect we all felt a bit disappointed over the attendance, and this regret, coupled with the loss of spontaneity, produced a less compelling liturgy. Although those who came on Sunday seemed genuinely surprised and pleased with "Motherhood Reborn," we felt that our sense of timing had suffered. It is possible that such a liturgy should be a one-time affair.

There are three aspects of our experience with this particular liturgy which deserve special mention as indicating the power of collaboration and willingness to risk the untried:

1. The positive mood: the enthusiasm of the group permeated both the tone and the content of the liturgy.
2. The openness of involvement: the inclusion of talent from outside our own group, the threading-in of materials from the lectures as well as the workshops, and the rejection of exclusive participation.
3. The belief in human creativity: a sense of the dramatic unfolding of our persons where opportunity is offered.

The text which follows represents a combination of elements from both presentations.

MOTHERHOOD REBORN

CALL TO WORSHIP

Good morning. Today we are offering an alternative Mother's Day liturgy, which we have called "Motherhood Reborn," as an attempt to experience a fuller meaning of motherhood. Our understanding of motherhood refers to a theology of wholeness: the theology of the inclusion of the feminine in the Divine, and its location within ourselves. Four components of the feminine are called to mind: grounding, creating, nuturing, and delivering. Grounding is understood as the confident finding of ourselves in the "I am"; creating, as the unbounded beginnings and possibilities of each of us and the opportunity for community; nurturing, as the supportiveness and trust which comes with community; and delivering, as our liberation from ingenuous expectations and stereotypes toward humanity and totality.

CREDAL STATEMENT *(in unison)*

> We affirm God—grounding our existence, affirming our identity as sisters in Christ;
>
> We affirm God—creating a spirit of newness and life in each of us;
>
> We affirm God—nurturing our confidence, caring for one another;
>
> We affirm God—delivering us beyond ourselves, freeing ourselves.

The first line of the Credal Statement was then sung, solo with guitar improvisation; this was done throughout the service.

AFFIRMATION—GROUNDING

READINGS: Genesis 1:27; Galatians 3:27–28

READING: Speech of Sojourner Truth

Here the mother and daughter walked to the altar and placed a pot and a plant next to each other.

SONG

AFFIRMATION—CREATING

CORPORATE RESPONSE

> We are created in the image of God,
> Born of God to give birth to love, understanding, freedom, the personhood of all people.
> Let us not forget God who gave us birth.

READINGS: Deuteronomy 32:17–18; Judges 5:6,7,12

READING BY THE DAUGHTER: "Have a Nice Day"

Here the mother and daughter again walked to the altar, and the young girl planted the plant while the mother held the pot for her.

AFFIRMATION—NURTURING

LET US NOT FORGET GOD WHO GAVE US BIRTH

READING: Deuteronomy 32:10–11

(With a brief word of introduction on the shifting of the pronouns he *to* she, *and* him *to* them *on the basis of feminine imagery.)*

DANCE LITURGY

(Performed by men and women; dance represented chaos and creation, with movement of eagle swooping and swirling as protective "finale.")

READING: Hosea 11:1–4

STATEMENT: "a personal reflection on motherhood"
". . . Motherhood is the first experience I have had of total commitment. Through my commitment to mothering Genevieve I learned

about the responsibility involved in making other commitments.

"Motherhood taught me the value of sharing experiences, both good and bad, with others. It was in sharing my fears, ignorance, and weakness with other mothers that I learned to value the support of other people. I found that a mother who is confident about herself is more important to a child than the food a baby eats. . . .

"The commitment, sharing, and skills learned from the experience of mothering are helpful for all of us. Those of us who are mothers know this first hand. Those of us who would be mothers have learned it someplace, but all of us have been in contact with the wisdom which comes with the experience of motherhood."

A student walked to the altar and watered the plant.

SONG: "Love One Another"

AFFIRMATION—DELIVERING

READING: a personal "theological reflection"
"For me as a woman to experience God is to experience a breaking forth . . . a liberation . . . a delivering. It occurs within me, with a me which is grounded so that it can enter into relationship with integrity, self-worth, and freedom.
"God is experienced as the synergy . . . the coming together . . . of pain and birthing, of death and resurrection, of fragmentation and wholeness. God is birthing that occurs within and among us.
"Nurturance is the 'BEING WITH' aspect of this bursting forth process. TO BE WITH another is to nurture . . . it is to truly HEAR the

birthing. We hear birthings through movement, through physical touch, and through affirming expressions of oneness. The hearing links me with the other.

"Grounding, birthing, nurturing: together they constitute *delivering*—the liberating, transforming experience of grace. "To be delivered is to experience wholeness."

CORPORATE RESPONSE
In the fullness of ourselves, then we will be liberated!

OPEN LITANY

From a member of the class: "Personal liberation means moving from the position of saying no to things that are new and different—out of suspicion, possibly jeopardy—and turning toward the affirming: to say yes, I'll try. Today is a good example of overcoming hesitance, becoming a principal in an activity that is new for me, and, as it happens, very nourishing."

From a woman who came to the liturgy: "There is something liberating about seeing and hearing women together praise creation and creativity. I'm overjoyed to have been here and moved to get up and speak."

After some ten or more testimonials, the guitar strummed another song and people began to sing. In the middle of the singing one woman in a front bench walked out and approached another woman halfway back and took her hand; they left together and many others followed in a similar way.

Rose Arthur read the Call to Worship; Carolyn Hudson improvised on the guitar; Jaqueline Meadows led our dance liturgy class; Ann Squires presented her "personal reflection on motherhood"; Karen Bloomquist read her own "theological reflection"; Robin Casteel-Dowdle performed two of the vocal solos.

3

BRIT KEDUSHA:

A HOME CEREMONY CELEBRATING THE BIRTH OF A DAUGHTER

Ellen and Dana Charry

In creating this ceremony, we have tried to supply something which we feel is missing in Jewish life. Our Law requires the formal induction of every male child into the Jewish people through the ritual *Brit Mila* (Circumcision), a distinctive ceremony. This ancient rite, dating from the time of Abraham, is performed on the eighth day after the baby boy is born, usually in the child's home. The simple operation is performed by a *mohel* (ritual circumciser), who leads the ceremony which includes the naming of the child and blessings for him and his parents. The ceremony is held with friends and relatives in attendance, but without the mother, who is usually "protected" from watching the circumcision of her son. The ceremony is usually followed by a celebration. Although one of our shortest rituals, the *Brit Mila* is certainly one of the most powerful and unforgettable.

Two other religious customs accompany the birth of a son in Jewish tradition. One is *Pidyon ha-Ben* (Redemption of the Firstborn), and the other is *Ben Zachar* (literally, Male Child). *Pidyon ha-Ben* is a brief ceremony reenacting the ancient custom of dedicating the firstborn male to the service of the temple. The child is "bought back" or redeemed from this sacred obligation by his father, who gives a symbolic sum of money to the temple priest. The *Ben Zachar* is simply a party, often given by the baby's grandparents, celebrating his arrival. All of these are home ceremonies, and not part of a synagogue service.

It is striking to us that there is no special ceremony to mark the birth of a female child. There is a practice of naming girls in the synagogue, but this is a custom, not required by Law. The father goes to the synagogue on the Sabbath following the baby's birth and is given a special honor during the reading of the Torah (Law). A blessing is added for the baby girl which includes a naming formula. Blessings such as this are recited on many other occasions also. Thus, the naming is not a distinct ceremony and has very little impact or special flavor to it. Its importance is further diminished by the fact that mother and daughter are usually not present. It should be noted that such a practice can be done for a boy child as well.

In short, there is a great disparity between the ceremonies for greeting the birth of a son and the practices attending the birth of a daughter. This inequality, with its implied value judgment, seemed to us distasteful, unbecoming to the Jewish tradition which we value so highly. Although understandable in historical perspective, the situation seems strangely out of place today. It is also jarringly dissonant with the love we feel for our daughters, the pride we take in them, and the expectations we have for their future. These are some of the feelings which moved us to create this new ceremony for celebrating the birth of a daughter.

This is not meant to be a female version of the *Brit Mila.* We have adapted one passage—the naming formula—from the *Brit Mila,* but in all other respects we have tried to create a distinct ceremony for girls.

Concepts exist only in thought. To become part of life, a concept must be given some concrete form. Thus, every ritual of Jewish life is associated with tangible ceremonial objects, and this new ceremony is no exception. Here, a Kiddush cup (ritual wine cup) is given to the baby. We selected the Kiddush cup for several reasons. Kiddush is the blessing over wine which sanctifies almost every Jewish ritual and religious holiday. It is included in *Brit Mila,* marriage, Sabbath, and all holy days. As a constant part of family ritual, the Kiddush represents ongoing Jewish tradition as we hope our children will experience it. In addition, the cup can be used from childhood through adulthood. Finally, the giving of a Kiddush cup expresses our hope that the full range of Jewish experience will always be open to our daughters. This is not true at the present time, as much of Jewish ritual observance is customarily denied to women.

We wrote the *Brit Kedusha* in anticipation of the birth of our second child. In concentrating our efforts to create something new and exciting, almost revolutionary in terms of Jewish tradition, we sought to preserve the flavor and language of the tradition while giving it new meaning. Therefore we were careful to include such elements as a traditional psalm, the blessing over wine, and the blessing for special occasions. These are all established parts of Jewish liturgy which we have here combined in a new way.

The title of the ceremony reflects two of our people's most vital ideas. *Kedusha* is usually translated as "holiness," but it also encompasses the ideas of uniqueness, specialness, and spirituality. All of Judaism expresses the idea of *Kedusha,* and every Jewish act is a striving toward the goal. *Brit* means a contract, covenant, or pact between man and God. The Bible uses the word to describe the agreement between Abraham and God—

as symbolized by the Circumcision ritual—and between God and the whole Jewish people—as symbolized by the giving of the Law at Sinai. The word *Brit* also represents the long chain of tradition and learning which stretches across the generations to the present day, constantly reworking and revitalizing that ancient covenant.

In their striving toward *Kedusha,* we hope that our children will add a new link to the living chain of the *Brit.*

Our ceremony was held eight days after the baby was born. Before the ceremony, we chose the cup we would give our daughter and had it engraved with her name and date of birth. Her Kiddush cup was of medium size, so that she could not only use it as a baby but also as she grows up.

On the day of the ceremony the room was arranged with places at the front for ourselves, our parents, our three-year-old daughter, and several other relatives and friends who had parts in the ceremony. The rest of the guests sat facing us. In front of our places a small table was set up, on which the new Kiddush cup and a bottle of wine were placed.

We felt that the ceremony needed a leader, and we designated certain parts in the text to be read by the leader. Ideally the leader should not be one of the parents. But when we performed the ceremony for the first time we took some of the leader's parts ourselves and distributed the rest to several close friends and relatives. In addition we wanted to demonstrate the fact that the leader need not be a rabbi. A rabbi is basically a teacher. He is the outstanding leader of the community and is regarded as more learned than the lay population in deciding questions of Jewish Law. Although his presence is not required for any liturgical ceremony of Jewish life, it is customary in most synagogues that the

rabbi and/or the cantor conduct the service. We felt
that our ceremony could be led instead by any knowl-
edgeable and sensitive layperson.

The ceremony was originally written in Hebrew, the
language of the Jewish liturgy. Use of the traditional
Hebrew conveyed the feeling that this new ceremony
was very much in keeping with the spirit of Jewish
tradition. Since many Jews these days are unable to
read or understand Hebrew, we followed each section
in our liturgy with an English translation. In perform-
ing the ceremony we did each part first in Hebrew, then
in English. For this English volume we have omitted
the Hebrew altogether.

BRIT KEDUSHA

*The guests having assembled, the grandparents took their places
at the front and the parents then entered with the baby and
took their seats.*
One of our friends recited:

> Sing out to God, all the earth,
> Break forth and sing for joy.
> Sing praises to God with the harp,
> And with voices full of joyous melody.
> With trumpets and the sound of the horn
> Sing out to God.
>
> Let the sea roar in all its fullness,
> The whole world and all its inhabitants.
> Let the floods clap their hands,
> And the mountains sing for joy
> Before God and the nations. *(Ps. 98)*

The grandparents:

> We praise you, O Lord our God, who has kept us
> alive, and strengthened us, and permitted us to see
> this day.

(This is the traditional blessing said on all special or unique occasions.)

Dana's sister, who had come from Israel, then took the baby in her arms and said:

Our God and God of our people, sustain this child along with her mother and father. Let her name be called in Israel:

Tamar Yael Debora
daughter of Ellen and Dana Charry

May the father and mother rejoice with their child, as it is written, "Let your parents be happy. Let your mother thrill with joy." *(adapted from* Brit Mila)

She then returned the child to us and we said:

Our God and God of our people—
May the life of this child be one of happiness, goodness, and wisdom.
Grant that she may seek after peace and pursue an end to strife among her fellowmen.

Strengthen us to guide our daughter in the path of our Torah and its beliefs.
Help us to lead her in the footsteps of the great leaders of Israel, whose deeds continue to shine across the ages of our people.

We praise you, O God, whose Torah links the generations one to another. *(original)*

This is a point in the ceremony where the leader may speak informally. The leader may, for example, add a personal prayer, express personal hopes for the child, or say something about the significance of the baby's name. In the case of our daughter, each of us spoke for several minutes. We explained the background of the ceremony, expressing many of the ideas set forth above in our prefatory comments. We held up the Kiddush cup for all to see, and filled it with wine. We then chanted together:

> We praise you, O Lord our God, who has created the fruit of the vine. *(this is the Kiddush)*

We then stood with the baby and, placing our hands on her head, blessed her with the following traditional blessing:

> May you be blessed in the city and blessed in the country,
> May you be blessed as you enter and blessed as you depart.
>
> May God bless you and keep you,
>
> May He cause His face to shine upon you and be gracious to you.
>
> May He lift up His face to you and grant you wholeness and peace.

In conclusion, we and our older daughter recited the blessing, and all the guests joined in:

> We praise you, O Lord our God, who has kept us alive, and strengthened us, and permitted us to see this day.

We then went on to eat, drink, and celebrate.

The ceremony was received with great enthusiasm. All of those present, without exception, felt that they had witnessed something beautiful and innovative. A close friend of ours commented that she found it hard to believe the ceremony was brand new, since its language and spirit fit so well into our tradition.

4

A MASS FOR FREEDOM FOR WOMEN

C. Virginia Finn

Together with several other members of the local group of St. Joan's Alliance, I have participated thus far in the construction of three Mass liturgies, all specifically feminist and intended to raise the consciousness level of the faithful. I have also been actively involved in a liturgy-planning group which is not specifically feminist; here too, though, my own consciousness operates in such a way as to eliminate aspects of the liturgy which limit women or ignore them.

My perception of the eucharistic sacrifice is that it is prayer. My experience in planning liturgies has taught me that communal prayer is a more difficult and a different thing than individual prayer. Three things—lack of training, inexperience, and not knowing what to expect—made parts of the planning process for some of these liturgies painful. However, the spiritual perceptions which resulted were always worth the pain.

The liturgy presented here was originally intended to commemorate the fifty-third anniversary of the ratifying of the Nineteenth Amendment to the United States Constitution granting women citizens the right to vote. It was used August 26, "Women's Rights Day," and the congregation at St. Michael's Church in Mil-

waukee knew in advance that this would be the theme
of the celebration.

Specific themes are not unusual for this congregation,
which is not large, varies in size from Sunday to Sunday, and for several years now has been involving all
who wished to be involved in the planning of liturgies.
Our people are accustomed to readings other than those
in the "missalette," and to taking part in dialogue-
homilies which are sometimes quite long. The Mass
frequently lasts seventy-five minutes, sometimes ninety,
occasionally only sixty.

Whenever the liturgy to be constructed is explicitly
intended to be feminist, or to deal honestly with the
status of women in the church, I approach the celebrant
in advance with a series of predetermined questions. I
ask my questions in a sequence that seems likely to
elicit the most "yes" answers from the outset. When
the celebrant begins to hesitate in answering, or seems
reluctant to answer, or says a flat "No!" I stop asking.
But I do attempt to bring up the remaining concerns
at some point during the ensuing discussion with the
celebrant. I do so for two reasons: first, to get his reaction, and second, to make it easier for the next feminist. Our hope is that once the questioning has begun,
the thought-reaction process will also have begun, and
that prayerful reflection will bring the desired change,
however slowly.

These are the questions I habitually ask and the
sequence in which I ask them:

May feminists construct the liturgy?

    Usually this question is expected and I'm regarded
    as somehow "behind the times" for even asking it.

May we use readings other than Scripture?

    Usually permission is granted, though a preference
    for Scripture may be expressed.

May women be lectors?

Usually this is granted without hesitation.

May we have a dialogue homily?

Celebrants vary in their opinions on this question.

May a woman give the homily?

Again, the celebrants vary.

May women serve at the altar?

Usually this is granted, but some celebrants evade the issue by deciding to do without servers, thereby denying any woman who wishes to serve the opportunity which she may not get elsewhere.

May we hang a banner which says . . . ?

Permission is usually given if the banner's statement connects with the liturgy.

May women distribute communion?

Celebrants vary; so does the manner of distribution.

May we delete words which refer to God as male?

The usual reaction is another question: "What would you use in their place?" When we answer, "Creator, Redeemer, Sanctifier," permission is usually granted.

May we feminize the pronouns which refer to people, with the understanding that "woman" implicitly includes "man"?

Most celebrants respond that such a thing is uncharitable to men; some even suspect us of vindictiveness, evidencing little sensitivity to the feelings of women after nineteen hundred years of similar treatment. If permission is denied, two roads are open: we use the terms *people* and *persons* throughout, or we insert female terms as *woman, girl, sister, daughter* alongside the corresponding male terms whenever needed. Indeed, placing the feminine term first in such pairings is a sure consciousness-raiser.

May we feminize references to God?

Usually the answer is "No," sometimes merely hesitation. A recourse is to eliminate the use of pronouns altogether, and keep proper terms; our language is likely to be strained as a result but this too can help to erode the prevailing attachment to phallic worship.

Reluctance about eliminating references to God as male seems to peak at the point of the "Our Father." Everyone loves the phrase; so do I. Nonetheless, the identity of God as male is precisely the identity from which we must pry ourselves loose: God is neither male nor female. Both female and male have been created in the image and likeness of God. Asserting this explicitly in the liturgy, which is our communal prayer life, is necessary if women are to be accorded their own independent being, their own souls.

Translators inform us that the biblical term *Abba* is a babbling term similar to *Dada;* it has been translated as "Father." The recognition that babbling is an activity of very young infants, however, eases the transition of the imagery from male to female. In ancient Hebrew culture the care of the children was most likely entrusted to the mother and a nursing mother or wet nurse. That is still the practice today. The image of God as nursing mother is not foreign to Catholic writing: Teresa of Avila, for example, uses it.

With this explanation, the well-known form of address in prayer can, without too much uneasiness, become "Our Mother." If the faith-level of the celebrant or the congregation still does not allow for acceptance of the "Our Mother," then we yield. The prayer is either retained in its traditional version or eliminated. It does not have to be in the Mass. In my experience, however, the "Our Father" is usually kept as is—which is OK with me, because I love it too.

A MASS FOR FREEDOM FOR WOMEN

ENTRANCE SONG: "It's a Long Road to Freedom"

OPENING GREETING

PRAYER OF THE FAITHFUL

Earlier this month, a "Liturgy Study Day" was held at St. Francis Seminary. The theme of the day was "How to make our traditions work for us." Our Church honors its traditions; yet some of these traditions are misleading and can malform the people of God. Notable among these are the attitudes of the Fathers of the church toward women:

From the tradition of Tertullian, who called women "the devil's gateway," and said they should dress in mourning and repentance so that they may more fully expiate the ignominy of the first sin,

Free us, O Lord.

From the tradition of Clement of Alexandria who said that nothing for man is disgraceful, for man is endowed with reason; but for woman it brings shame even to reflect of what nature she is,

Free us, O Lord.

From the tradition of Cyril of Alexandria who said the female sex is "death's deaconess" and is especially dishonored by God,   *Free us, O Lord.*

From the tradition of John Damascene who described woman as the advanced post of hell, *Free us, O Lord*

From the tradition of Ambrose who said, "She who does not believe is a woman and should be designated by the name of her sex, whereas she who believes progresses to perfect manhood, to the measure

of the adulthood of Christ, and then dispenses with
the name of the sex,"   *Free us, O Lord.*

From the tradition of Thomas Aquinas who called
women "misbegotten men" and held them useful
only for procreation,   *Free us, O Lord.*

From the traditions which teach our priests to fear
women as temptations and therefore prevent some
of them from serving one-half the people of God,
                              Free us, O Lord.

This we ask through Christ, our Lord,   *So be it.*

Reconciliation Rite

We, the teaching church, have permitted our word-
imagery to mislead us.
    Lord, have mercy. *Lord, have mercy.*
We, the people of God, have stereotyped ourselves
and hurt one another.
    Christ, have mercy. *Christ, have mercy.*
God, our creator, who can be Mother as well as
Father, help us to free ourselves as a people and
our church as an institution.
    Lord, have mercy. *Lord, have mercy.*
May almighty God have mercy on us, forgive us our
sins, and bring us to everlasting life. *So be it.*

Simple Doxology

Opening Prayer

A prophet is never without honor, except in her
own country. Let's take "prophet" in the sense of
one who speaks for another and pray that we
may remain mindful of what we say to one another
because of our own different social involvements.
We bear witness to, and for, one another, and so
become a people who care for one another. We ask
this through Christ our Lord.   *So be it.*

LITURGY OF THE WORD

FIRST READING: the story of Sojourner Truth and her
   famous speech in Akron, Ohio
   So spoke Sojourner Truth.

PSALM RESPONSE: Fiat. It may be done to me.

> *Fiat. It may be done to me.*

> You answered alone
> you did not run
> to Joseph or Anne
> or the temple men.

> *Fiat. It may be done to me.*

> You answered alone
> yet you are the one
> they claim as a model
> to keep us from
> answering
> alone.

> *Fiat. It may be done to me.*

SECOND READING: an excerpt from the diary of St.
   Catherine of Siena. Catherine protested when she was
   told by God to heal the Great Schism:
   "How shall it be done with me as You have said? For
   my sex is an obstacle as You know, Lord . . . because
   it is contemptible in men's eyes. . . . But the Lord
   answered, 'I pour out the favor of my Spirit on
   whom I will. There is neither male nor female . . .
   high or low. All are equal before me. . . . Therefore,
   my daughter, it is my will that you appear before
   the public.' "

This is the Word of the Lord.   *Thanks be to God.*

GOSPEL ACCLAMATION: Alleluia.   *Alleluia.*

Jesus said to her, " . . . Go to my brothers and tell them for me . . . ." (*John 20:16–17*) *Alleluia.*

GOSPEL: Luke 18:1–5

DIALOGUE-HOMILY

LITURGY OF THE EUCHARIST

OFFERTORY SONG: "Joy is Like the Rain"

The Mass continued in the usual format, except that references to "people" were feminized, as in the following:

EUCHARISTIC PRAYER

Creator, we acknowledge your greatness: all your actions show your wisdom and love. You formed woman in your own likeness and set her over the whole world to serve you, her creator, and to rule over all creatures. Even when she disobeyed you and lost your friendship, you did not abandon her to the power of death, but helped all women to seek and find you. Again and again you offered a covenant to woman, and through the prophets taught her to hope for salvation. . . .

COMMUNION SONG: "Spirit of God"

COMMEMORATIVE MENTION

We asked for this theme for this Mass because today, August 26th, is the fifty-third anniversary of the ratifying of the Nineteenth Amendment to the United States Constitution, which recognized women's right to vote. We wish to express our thanks to St. Michael's Parish and to Father Thomas LeMieux, our celebrant, and particularly to acknowledge the women who struggled and persevered for the Nineteenth Amendment, and we pray that all of us, women and men alike, may exhibit similar faith in ourselves.

The poem *Fiat* was written by Joan Krofta. Sister Jeanne Richardson led the dialogue-homily.

5

A CELEBRATION on the OPENING of the ECUMENICAL WOMEN'S CENTERS

EWC Planning Group

The Ecumenical Women's Centers in Chicago were formed by women from various Christian confessional groups who had a concern about women's liberation theology and women's role in church and society. The liturgy presented here was used as part of a two-day celebration of their opening.

The first day of the celebration people gathered to view "Eve 'n Us," a three-part slide show telling of the Judeo-Christian tradition concerning women, and to share in a dialogue with the Reverend Peggy Way. On the second day we celebrated the opening and commissioned the Reverend Floris Mikkelsen as the Centers' first Coordinator.

To commemorate the opening of the EWC we wrote a liturgy which was to be a Christian celebration using nonsexist language and concepts—a challenging task. This liturgy, although planned by three women from the Centers, integrates parts of various liturgies from other feminist services.

As the three of us began to plan this service we had
several major concerns in mind: 1) using nonsexist
language and concepts; 2) having the group participate;
3) celebrating women's history; 4) recalling our corporate and personal heritages; 5) experiencing the tension of patriarchal tradition; 6) reinterpreting old
myths and images; 7) sharing hopes and visions for the
Centers; and 8) commissioning the first Coordinator.

We all agreed that the language and concepts to be
used had to be nonsexist. This not only gave us a problem in selecting the Scripture passage; it also made
all the early creeds of the church unusable without some
alteration. We selected a trinitarian formula developed
earlier for a Lutheran women's service: "In the name of
God, the mother and father of all life. . . ." This termi-
nology represented an attempt on our part to use some
old formulations wherever possible.

The three of us desired a form that would allow and
encourage as much group participation as possible. As
a result the service consisted almost entirely of unison
or responsive readings. We found that the people were
eager to participate and responded very well.

We wanted to plan a service that celebrated women's
history and images. Knowing that both women and
men had been invited, however, we felt it necessary
to do this in a service in which men too could freely
participate.

We felt the need for recalling our corporate heritage
as women. We wanted also to recall our personal histories, particularly our relationships with women who
had been important in our lives. We lifted up the names
of people like Joan Baez, Eleanor Roosevelt, and our
own mothers.

Since the three of us had been closely related to the
church all our lives, we felt the need to acknowledge
our struggle with the patriarchal Judeo-Christian tradi-

tion even while trying to reclaim it for our own participation. The Prayer of Confession served as a way of expressing that tension.

As we struggled with this tradition which continually denies our personhood, yet at the same time had been important in liberating us, we felt the need to reinterpret the old myths and images. The "Liberation of the Apples" was one attempt at reinterpretation as was the new trinitarian formula in the Invocation. "Daughters of God," rewritten as a parody of the hymn "Sons of God," was another example of how we altered only some of the original material, but it was an alteration that gave the song a totally new meaning for us as women.

As this was a special service for many of us who had worked hard to see the Centers come into being, we wanted a time when hopes and visions for the Centers could be spoken and celebrated corporately. This happened at the end of the section entitled "Celebrating a New Humanity," when people were encouraged to lift up possibilities.

Since we had just hired a full-time staff woman and wanted to be in a covenant relationship with her, the commissioning part of the service was integral. We read the group covenant and then individuals had an opportunity during the laying on of hands to make additional commitments.

Some of these eight concerns were verbalized and talked about repeatedly during the planning, while others were less concrete or not articulated. We did not sit down and outline our concerns on paper. We simply talked about our ideas of worship and shared specific feelings or concepts that we should like to include. Then we drew heavily on our experiences with other feminist services that we had helped to plan or had participated in.

There were a few problems and some moments of

confusion as most of the service was a new experience for many of the people. In the "Liberation of the Apples," for example, people were not sure whether to read as they ate the apples, to eat the whole apple first and then read, or perhaps just to have a bite and then read. Although clearer instructions would have been helpful, this part of the service added to the reinterpretation of old myths.

The public announcement of the Celebration included an invitation to all, so we did not know how many men might attend. Since only a few men came, the reading of the men's parts made them a bit uncomfortable. It might have been helpful if we had planned in advance to have a number of men on hand prepared to lead in the reading of the men's parts.

This liturgy was created mainly to celebrate the opening of the Ecumenical Women's Centers. The commissioning of the EWC Coordinator was integral to the celebration, but not its central or major element. The idea of a covenanting service, however, for a group of people planning to work together with one another and their staff is a good one. We felt that it proved important to our later common endeavors.

A CELEBRATION on the OPENING of the ECUMENICAL WOMEN'S CENTERS

INVOCATION

Liturgist: In the name of God, the mother and father of all life, in the name of the Son, who liberates us, and in the name of the Spirit who keeps us going with love and power.

People: We celebrate your presence as we worship together. We also celebrate our presence because we are glad to be here to share our humanness and our faith. It's great to be alive!

LITANY OF THANKSGIVING FOR OUR SISTERS

Liturgist: We commemorate women in the Bible who were strong leaders and servants:

> Old Testament women who demonstrated their faith in Yahweh,
>
> New Testament women who showed their love for Christ,
>
> Esther, who risked her life so that her people could live,
>
> Mary Magdalene, who was the first witness to Christ's resurrection.

People: Help us follow their example of faith and love.

Liturgist: We also remember women in the past who lived what they believed in:

> Sojourner Truth, a former slave who became an abolitionist and feminist orator;
>
> Harriet Tubman, a black slave woman who gained her freedom and then organized the underground railroad that brought three hundred women, men, and children out of bondage;

Elizabeth Cady Stanton and Susan B. Anthony, who for fifty years, planned, organized, and strategized for the women's movement until it became a national force.

People: They struggled for freedom. Help us to struggle, Lord, and to learn and grow as we struggle, not only for our own personal freedom, but for freedom for all people.

Liturgist: We also remember beautiful women of today who have not forgotten how to smile, laugh, dance, sing, and celebrate:
who continue to struggle,
who have meaningful lives,
who help sisterhood bloom,
who listen and cry and drink coffee together.

People: Thank you, Lord, we rejoice with these women.

Liturgist: Let us also remember special women in our lives:

Let the people share their witnesses; after each witness the people respond:

People: Thank you, Lord, we rejoice for this woman.

LIBERATION OF THE APPLES (*in unison*)
As we share in the eating of these apples—
We reject Man's traditional interpretation of the Adam and Eve story.
We affirm that the story does not convey truth to us about apples and certainly not about ourselves.
We hold that Eve performed the first free act.
We pledge ourselves to communicate and to collaborate in developing the human tradition, the whole truth, for the liberation of the whole family and all creation.

PRAYER OF CONFESSION (*in unison*)

Our Father, even as we call you "Father" we are mindful of the dominance of masculinity in our society and church. We confess our propensity to define the ultimate as masculine, and to relegate the feminine to a lesser status. We painfully acknowledge the role of women as underlings and objects, and we deplore the exploitation of women in our society. Hasten the day when it will be as OK to be a woman as it is to be a man. And bring all of us, we pray, into a deeper and larger vision in which male and female are both remembered as a part of that original creation which you looked upon as good, indeed as very good. Amen.

THE GOOD NEWS AS LUKE REMEMBERED IT: Luke 4:16–19

THE CELEBRATION OF THE CENTERS

1. Celebration of the New Humanity

Female Liturgist: We as women are strong.

We as women are powerful.

We as women can do things.

Women: Liberation is ours for the claiming.

Female Liturgist: We need to be more in touch with our strength, our power, and our capabilities.

We need to be free to be ourselves.

We need not stifle our God-given talents.

Women: The gospel is liberation.

Female Liturgist: We don't have to stay in our place.

Women: The gospel frees us from the law.

Female Liturgist: Jesus broke law and tradition in his treatment of women.

Women: Jesus was a feminist!

Male Liturgist: When you are free, then we are freer.

We don't have to prove our manliness.

We don't have to prove our "natural superiority."

We don't have to claim anything.

Men: Liberation is ours for the claiming.

Male Liturgist: We need to be more in touch with our tears.

We need to be free to be ourselves.

We need to discard our "masculine role" and discover who we really are.

Men: The gospel is liberation.

Male Liturgist: We are free to share our responsibilities.

Men: The gospel frees us from the law.

Male Liturgist: Jesus challenged the status quo.

Men: Jesus calls us to full humanity.

All: We reject the notion that one sex should build bridges and the other keep the home fires burning.

We reject the idea of "proper roles," for roles belong to the realm of law, and freedom belongs to the gospel.

We believe the words of the New Testament that in God's time and place there is no male and female, no mankind or womankind, no manhood or womanhood, but simply humanhood, simply God's people.

We can and will be more human.

We will find ways of being men and women together.

2. Litany

Left: I will not bow down before a god who has men pray, "I thank you Lord that you have not created me a woman."

Right: I will not worship a god who entrusts his priesthood and his power and his prophecy only to men.

Left: I will not serve a god for whom woman was unclean for twice as long when she bore a girl child, or a god for whom a woman's mission is to listen and a man's mission is to speak.

All: You are not my god, Jehovah!

Right: Let us look into these things. The human spirit is to be a soaring one which stands on the abyss, yet affirms what or to whom its bondage is to be.

Left: I will not have my spirit and my nature so identified that I cannot soar! I will not live with a sexed nature anymore.

Right: You are not my god, Jehovah, who will recognize me only by my sexual function. My brothers are measured by other standards than their sexuality, and their moral value is not limited to procreative roles.

All: I will not have a god who will not have me *whole*. I am a body and a mind. I am a womb and a soul. I am a wife and a spirit. I am a mother and a person.

Women: What am I to do with a god who knows of women only as harlots or virgins? as tempters or cloistered? as playgirls or nonpersons to be placed upon religious pedestals?

All: I do not know which is the greater insult to my creation: to be forever a daughter of Eve whom men fear through their sin-obsession; or to be forever pedestaled, protected from the storms and stresses and creativities and responsibilities of human development which produce persons and adults.

Women: You are not my god, Jehovah. I will speak
with my brothers. I will affirm my sisters. I will
cry unto my God, "'Let us free one another!"
I will speak with my brothers, "I will call you
brother even though you will not call me sister,
for we must love one another or die, we must be
partners in the created order over which the
human persons, man and woman, were given
dominion." I will speak with my brothers, "I
will go into your secret places and your sanctu-
aries where you hide from a partnership, where
the prophets gather and the priests, where the
kings govern and the pure minds teach, where
the courts define and the generals fight. I will go
into your secret places and discover there your
hidden mysteries. And I will say, 'I am a stranger
and afraid in a world I never made, where I cannot breathe your air, nor save our sons from
your wars; nor protect our daughters from your
person–empty principles; nor with my black
brothers and sisters enter your institutions,
where I cannot govern my country or community, nor even minister among my sisters.' I do not
need to claim that I could do a better job! But
do you sense no need for me, for my resources,
competence, and creativity? For I will affirm that
I too was created with the image of God within
me! We will affirm our uniqueness among ourselves, sisters, and will give support to one
another. And as we are becoming, we may free
our brothers too."

All: I will cry unto my God, "Let us free one
another!" Amen.

3. Possibilities

Liturgist: Let us lift up the possibilities we see in

LET US FREE ONE ANOTHER!

SANDY BAUER '74

THE COMMISSIONING OF THE NEW COORDINATOR

the new center. (*People may share their hopes.*)
COVENANT (*in unison*)
We covenant with you and with one another to
be a faithful community as we share in the new
life of the Centers, together identifying issues
and responding to the task ahead of us.

THE LAYING ON OF HANDS

(*People may say whatever seems appropriate.*)

SONG: "Daughters of God"

LOVE FEAST

(*The bread and wine are shared with the nearest person.*)

SONG: "One in the Spirit" (*substituting "one" for "man"*)

GOING FORTH

The New Coordinator: May you receive the power and
the strength to minister to and with others, freeing
each other to be open to and participants in the
creation of new life.

All: Let us go in peace.

Sources for this liturgy:
Invocation: Lutheran Women's Service, Chicago, Feb. 27, 1972.
Litany of Thanksgiving: adapted from the same Lutheran Women's
Service.
Liberation of the Apples: Grailville, Ohio, Women's Conference,
Summer, 1972.
Prayer of Confession: Union Theological Seminary, New York, 1972.
Celebration of the New Humanity: by Tilda Norberg, received in
resource material of the United Church of Christ for Reformation
Sunday, 1972.
Litany: adapted from Peggy Way's sermon, Chicago, 1970.
Going Forth: Floris Mikkelsen's ordination, Oakland, California, 1970.

6

SISTERCELEBRATION:

TO CULTIVATE THE GARDEN

Maurine Stephens

"Sistercelebration" was an ecumenical worship service commemorating the fifty-third anniversary of the ratification of the woman's suffrage amendment to the United States Constitution on August 26, 1920.

The idea of having a worship service as the focus for observing the occasion, which fell on a Sunday, came from the local chapter of the National Organization for Women. NOW asked our Philadelphia Task Force on Women and Religion (a support and action group which publishes a national bimonthly newsletter called *Genesis III*) if we would be willing to plan such a service. We were not only willing but eager and excited about the possibilities. Thus it was that Philadelphia's first city-wide worship service planned by women, led by women, and intended primarily for women to celebrate a milestone in the history of the movement for feminism and social justice, went to the drawing boards. We had only about five weeks to prepare it, which meant that we would have to work fast.

From the beginning the service was conceived as a collective effort in both its planning and execution. We felt that none of us alone had the creativity or resources available to several of us working together. Then, too, we all wanted the service itself to be a model of leadership-sharing, and we especially did not want to lend support to the worship model in which an ordained person is the leader and those not ordained are excluded from leadership.

As one of the ordained women, I agreed to serve as coordinator for the planning group. We first nailed down the time of service, settling on 2 P.M. as a convenient time which would not conflict with regular Sunday church services. As for a place, we wanted a downtown location, with a church being the most obvious choice. We were fortunate in being warmly welcomed by the minister of the first church we contacted, a beautiful and historic Presbyterian church.

The first planning session occurred as a brainstorming session in connection with a conference on women and theology sponsored at the end of July by the Task Force. One of the ideas which emerged here was that we develop the service around a central symbolic act in which everyone would participate, a community-creating act.

This idea forced us to think through the nature of our potential congregation—who we hoped would come and who was likely to come—and also to decide what we wanted the service to do and to be, starting simply with the anniversary occasion itself. Of course, we had to decide what we meant by calling this event a "worship" service, beyond the fact that we would be holding it on a Sunday in a church building.

That brainstorming session also gave us the name for our service. "Sistercelebration" we hoped would intrigue and invite people as well as give some clue about what the event was to be.

Having no single group for a congregation, and a potential congregation drawn from all over the city and its suburbs, we knew it could be extremely important to get out the word. We worked hard on developing an effective publicity program. NOW used its resources and contacts to get posters printed, newspapers informed, announcements disseminated through the NOW newsletter, and radio and TV stations contacted. Ruth Duck of the Task Force designed a symbol for the service: a clenched fist inside the woman symbol forming the core of an apple with one bite missing. We distributed a couple of hundred posters, mailed out flyers to churches and women's groups, and printed up about four hundred programs—far more than we expected to need for the service, in order that we might have some available later. The day before the service I was interviewed on a radio program, and several newspapers mentioned the upcoming service, one of them carrying a lengthy article on the subject.

We felt that our hard work on publicity paid off, because we had a group of at least a hundred eager and expectant people—including several men and children —gathered at Old Pine Street Church at 2 o'clock, most of them unknown to us. And this was the last weekend in August, not the most auspicious time to try to get people together in the city! Much to my surprise, we also had three TV camera crews on hand hoping to film the service. We had decided beforehand that filming during the service itself would distract us and the congregation from our purpose. We stood firm, therefore, and were amazed to find that, instead of leaving, the TV people stayed for the service, watching from the rear of the church. Afterward they filmed people outside as they were leaving. They filmed the sanctuary inside as we had rearranged and decorated it for the service, and they conducted interviews with several of us who had been involved in the service—all of which appeared on the news that evening.

In addition to providing publicity, our group's next step was to design the service itself. I worked on a skeletal outline, borrowing from Roman Catholic theologian Rosemary Ruether the idea of cultivating the garden earth. It seemed to express the vision of the feminist spirit. The call to worship was to be a call to celebration, very brief, including an acknowledgment of our purpose in gathering together in this particular place on this particular day, together with a few words about the service itself—that it would be informal, that our hope was that everyone would participate fully, and that we would not allow the rigid structure of the pews to determine our mood and restrict our movement. As it worked out, that introduction, following a "prelude" of taped rock music—and the prior distribution to arriving worshipers of bongos, cymbals, tambourines, and other children's musical instruments borrowed from "Get Set" centers—did in fact loosen folks up and let them know that they were not to expect a traditional service.

The outline went on to a Declaration to be read in lieu of any affirmation of faith, in which I tried to express some of the experiences and hopes of the congregation and the worship leaders. The purpose was to build and express community, not to divide and exclude.

The next element was called Sharing Our Struggle. We felt that in order to celebrate and affirm we needed first to confess, to acknowledge our hangups in order that we could then let go of them and move on. But we felt that confession had to be redefined in order to make sense in our service. Someone suggested that we divide people into groups of three and spend a few minutes in close conversation, each one sharing something about her or his own personal struggle or journey into liberation, to which the other two would respond, "We hear you and accept your struggle." Confession and acceptance thus would be community acts.

The other major element in my proposed outline was a litany in which we would give thanks for and praise to women in our history who have been part of our struggle for liberation. Two of the planners volunteered to write the litany, leaving room for people to add the names of other women at the end of the litany.

With that much of an outline at our major planning meeting, we were able together to develop the rest of the service. We decided that communion would not be appropriate as our central symbolic act because it is exclusively Christian, and we were trying to make the service an expression of the Jewish as well as the Roman Catholic and Protestant faiths. (Unfortunately, because our Jewish members and friends were not in town and available for the service, it came to reflect primarily the Christian orientation of its planners.) We wanted a new symbolic act, and we found it in the suggestion that we present the myth of Lilith, either read or acted out or danced, followed by Liberating the Apple.

The myth of Lilith is an old Jewish story which has been receiving the attention of women theologians in recent years. In the version called "Applesource: The Coming of Lilith," which is the one we used, Lilith is the first woman God creates. She does not like Adam's treatment of her as a subordinate, so she simply leaves the garden. Whereupon God creates Eve, who proves to be much more amenable to her role. That is, until she happens to encounter Lilith one day, and the two of them share "their stories" and decide to reenter the garden together, where God and Adam wait, afraid.

With the Adam-Eve-apple story thus overturned, we decided to "liberate the apple," to make it a symbol of liberation instead of a symbol of guilt used to keep women humble and subordinate to men. We decided to give everyone a cutout of an apple on the back of which each one was to write the next concrete step she or he planned to take in her or his own liberation struggle. We would then invite the congregation to bring the apples up to the front of the church and pin them on a huge painted cutout tree. We felt that this act followed naturally from the story-sermon and also from the act of confession as we defined it. The benediction would follow.

The service worked beautifully. Somehow, all the details had been taken care of, despite the very broad parceling-out of responsibilities. The response of the people was overwhelmingly positive: a spontaneous joyous round of embraces, congratulations, and fervent expressions of gratitude and hope for similar liturgies in the future.

SISTERCELEBRATION: TO CULTIVATE THE GARDEN

MUSIC

CALL TO CELEBRATION

DECLARATION *(in unison)*
> We are people in the process of change, we are moving, we are on the way.
>
> We are seeking the promise of life and hope amid the symbols of our past and the experiences of our present.
>
> We seek wholeness—in our lives, in our relationships, in our community.
>
> We are Jewish, we are Christian, we claim no religious community, we are exploring the traditions for the word that resonates with our deepest hopes and experiences.
>
> We seek community—the sisterhood of man, the brotherhood of woman.
>
> We want to cultivate the garden earth, not participate in its rape.
>
> We want no part of power that is death-dealing, that dominates, oppresses, and kills. We want to partici-

pate in the power that is life-supporting, that is grounded in the sense of human solidarity.

We are moving, we are on the way, we celebrate our struggle.

SHARING OUR STRUGGLE

SONG

LITANY OF PRAISE AND THANKSGIVING

Let us remember, in our prayers of praise and thanksgiving to the God who makes us all one, those women who have been part of our personal histories and those women who have struggled alongside the men of history to fashion a new age of hope and unity. Let us pray.

1st Reader: For Miriam, shrewd and strong protectress of Moses, prophetess among the people, bard of the exodus, leader through the wilderness;

2nd Reader: For Naomi, who could perceive the working of the divine, even when it was not yet visible to others; and for Ruth, yours by adoption from a foreign culture, who is—for Jew and non-Jew alike— the very model of devoted love;

3rd Reader: For Susanna, victimized like countless unnamed others by the men who viewed her as an object rather than as a person, but who still maintained her virtue and faith in God and triumphed over villainy;

Community: We give you thanks, O God.

The litany, after giving thanks for such women as Teresa of Avila, Anne Hutchinson, and Sojourner Truth, concluded with mention of contemporary women.

1st Reader: For the millions of our sisters who were hanged or burned at the stake in Christian Europe from the fourteenth to the seventeenth centuries, and even in the American colonies—women who were denounced as witches because they dared to be different or to assert their independence, or simply because they were women, whose sexuality was considered the work of the Devil;

2nd Reader: For those of our sisters today who have left the religious institutions because they have found them to be oppressive, male-defined and male-dominated, and who base their faith on the truth they know in their hearts;

3rd Reader: For the hundreds of women pastors and theologians who are trying to turn the religious institutions around and return them to the Scriptures; for courageous women—including Peggy Way, Rosemary Ruether, Elizabeth Farians, and Mary Daly—who dare to explore a feminist theology for us all;

Community: For their courage in responding to the truth of your spirit, we thank you, O God.

Here the community was invited to add names to the litany.

Community: We give you thanks, O God.

Community: For all sisters everywhere who are bringing fullness and richness and integrity into our lives and our congregations, and through whom your promises are fulfilled, we thank you, O God, to whom be all praise and glory. Amen.

SONG

THE MYTH OF LILITH

SONG: "Free to be You and Me"

LIBERATING THE APPLE

SONG: "Lady of Birth"

1. In the dawn of the ages God created the earth,
   To all the creatures she gave birth,
   To the birds in the sky, to the deer in the wood,

and God said, "It is good, it is good."
Refrain:
>Good, good, whoever you may be
>I am the Lady of Birth said she
>And I'll care for you whoever you may be
>Yes, I am the Lady of Birth said she.

2. In the dew of the morning all God's work had been done,
   But she said to herself with the rising of the sun,
   "Only one thing is lacking on the earth so wide,
   'Tis the children of earth walking by my side."

3. She reached down and gathered up the clay in her hands,
   And she took and she shaped them, a woman and a man,
   She breathed into each of them a life-giving soul
   And she gave each a striving to be whole.

4. Tell me, are you astounded that we tell such a tale
   Or do you think that God is only male?
   Then, remember our symbols cannot touch God at all,
   And we've made God a man ever since the fall.

BENEDICTION

Participants in "Sistercelebration":

The Reverend Maurine D. Stephens is co-minister at the Christian Association at the University of Pennsylvania.

Sister Audrey Miller, C.D.P., is on the youth ministry staff of the United Church of Christ.

Nancy Krody is coordinator of the Philadelphia Task Force on Women and Religion.

LaVonne Althouse is editor of *Lutheran Women* and of *Women's Pulpit*.

The Reverend Jean Alexander has been assistant minister at First Methodist Church in Germantown.

Ruth Duck is a graduate of Chicago Theological Seminary.

Mattie I. Humphrey is a Philadelphia *Tribune* columnist and community worker.

The Rev. Judith Kelsey is pastor of a United Methodist congregation in Illinois.

7

THE TRIAL OF THE HALLOWEEN SIX

Carol Adams

At a summer conference on women doing theology sponsored by the Philadelphia Task Force on Women in Religion, there emerged the idea of holding some sort of feminist Halloween celebration. Knowing that St. Mary's Episcopal Church in Philadelphia had used the traditional rite of exorcism at Halloween for several years, we suggested that some of their people join with some of us in PTFWR to work together on such a service. We agreed that an exorcism would be a good medium for removing the fear of women which exists in all of us and has been exhibited historically in the horrifying persecution and killing of women as witches during the Middle Ages in Europe and during the seventeenth century in Salem, Massachusetts.

After some initial brainstorming, we decided that the best way to convey the facts of the witch persecutions was to reenact dramatically a Salem witch trial, using primary sources. Though we attempted to work collectively on it, and many of us read up on witches, the play was finally written and directed by one woman, Diane Loudin. *The Trial* points out the parallels between the oppression of women as witches and the sexism that exists today. It also shows our own complicity in scapegoating women.

The most original, important, and innovative part of our service, the play, lasted about half an hour and paved the way for what followed. About twenty-five women participated in it. The role of an Observer provided structure to the play and pointed out the true intentions of the witnesses. Six defendants were on trial, all representing different types of women charged with being a witch. The various people who betrayed them included a woman who was jealous of the independence of some of the other women, a man who had raped one of the women and then accused her of enticing him, and a man who had been refused by one of the women. The final witness was one of the "witches" herself who, ugly and scorned her entire life, finally experienced her day of glory on the witness stand. As one of the "witches" declared while being dragged from the courtroom, "Someday you shall know the truth and the truth shall set you free." That was the hope of the play, and of the liturgy—if not to communicate the truth, at least to point out some of the falsehoods which shape our daily life.

We envisioned a movement from *The Trial*, through the exorcism of the fear of women, into a celebration of strong women in our past and our own strengths. The Celebration presented problems in that we did not wish simply to reuse our earlier "Sistercelebration" (see the preceding chapter). Instead of a litany honoring famous women in our past, we decided to emphasize the fact that our history has been hidden from us, or, worse yet, denied us. Just as we have no primary sources from the witches themselves but only from their trials and their persecutors, many women have been written out of our history because their activities were not considered important. The Act of Thanksgiving was an attempt to discover our sisters in the past. We also wanted to add new dimensions to our portraits of the women of whom we had heard, women who have excelled in fields of activity where they were allowed to participate. For example, we know that Jane Addams was a social worker, but we do not know that she actively campaigned for the peace movement during World War I, or that Dorothea Dix invented an improved lifeboat. It is fun, exciting, and not really difficult to put together a litany such as this, for the resources are endless if one searches them out. A good place to begin is the three-volume *Notable American Women* or a short pamphlet published by Times Change Press called *Generations of Denial*. Many histories of women being published today contain interesting facts about little-known women. Gerda Lerner's books on women in history and Eleanor Flexner's *Century of Struggle* are good places to check.

Song is an important medium for celebrating women. We were fortunate to have "Wine, Women, and Song," a very talented singing group, taking part. They picked most of the songs we interspersed among the long list of names. There are many songs available for services; *The Liberated Woman's Songbook* includes a variety of them. Another possibility is to rewrite hymns the way Ruth Duck rewrote "Lady of Birth" from "Lord of the Dance," or to substitute words such as "Faith of Our Mothers."

We were interested in maintaining four principles: we wanted both an ecumenical service and a feminist service; we wanted to have maximum congregational participation; and we wanted to write and perform the service collectively. We succeeded in implementing some of these principles better than others. For the Act of Thanksgiving we had starred a different name on each program, so that when the names were read off the voices would come from various parts of the congregation. It was fun to hear men reading some of these names, and good to hear the pride in the voices of the women as they read. Gasps, laughter, and clapping accompanied the reading of these names.

Maintaining a collective process throughout was difficult. As the day came closer there were some of us who, because of job commitments, could not devote enough time to the service. Neither did we learn as much about the exorcism as we might have. Though the rest of the service was ecumenical, the exorcism is heavily orthodox Christian, and it took many people by surprise. We had no "dress rehearsal" beforehand, and consequently did not anticipate the sharp contrast between the rest of the service and the exorcism. If we had, we might have explained the exorcism in the context of the dramatic, the reenacting of another ritual—like our drama—from the past. Or we could have written our own exorcism.

In preparing a liturgy it is very important to know just who your congregation is. If it is drawn mainly from the existent membership of one church it may not be necessary to take the precautions we took. Our Sistercelebration had been mainly for women, but we knew that both men and women would be coming to our Halloween service. While planning it as a feminist service, therefore, we wanted to be sure not to alienate the men who attended. We consciously included a place for them in the service. Some men even helped with the planning. By oversight we neglected to point out in our service that it is the lesbians who today are placed in the same position as the witches of old— that of persecuted outcasts. Many of the women in our past and in our congregation were lesbians, and we had failed to devote any attention to them.

It is important to allow plenty of time for working on a liturgy; time pressure can be quite a hassle. It is also important not to overstructure the service; there must be opportunities for spontaneity. At the end of our service many people wanted "Wine, Women, and Song" to continue singing. Unfortunately, because we had not anticipated this, it did not occur. But the desire to continue the service indicated that the 250 people attending felt comfortable with it. The time of refreshment afterward was important because it allowed for immediate feedback, discussion, and congratulations. Many people came up and hugged us; there was much laughter and joy; and the spirit was definitely with us.

THE TRIAL OF THE HALLOWEEN SIX

PERFORMANCE OF *The Trial*

THE CONFESSION

We confess that we have all been captive to the masculine mystique and the feminine mystique. We have believed, either openly or somewhere deep within our psyches, that maleness is the measure of full humanity and femaleness in some mysterious way flawed. We confess that we have only begun to understand how much damage we have done to ourselves and to each other under the sway of this mystique. Allowing our sex to define and limit our possibilities, we have disowned those qualities and needs and feelings in ourselves which do not fit. Thus alienated from ourselves, we have invested others with power and responsibility which belong to us alone. We confess that we are afraid of otherness, in those of the opposite sex as well as in those of our own. And we are afraid of our own otherness, those parts in ourselves that we have split off and do not claim, experiencing them rather as acting upon us from without.

We confess that we stand in need of cleansing and purgation, in order that we might experience healing and wholeness. Amen.

THE EXORCISM

I adjure you, O creature of salt, by the living God, by the true God, by the holy God, by God who commanded you to be cast—by the prophet Elisha—into the water to heal the barrenness thereof, that you become salt exorcised for the health of believers: and bring to all who take of you soundness of soul and body, and let all vain imaginations, wickedness, and subtlety of the wiles of the devil, and every unclean spirit fly and depart from every place where you shall be sprinkled, adjured by the name of him who shall come to judge both the quick and the dead, and the world by fire. Amen.

This was followed, in traditional fashion, by the blessing of the water, and concluded with the following prayer:

O God who mightily preserves your creation; with fear and trembling we entreat you, O Lord, and we beseech you graciously to behold this creature of salt and water, mercifully shine upon it, hallow it with the dew of your loving-kindness: that wheresoever it shall be sprinkled, with the invocation of your holy name, all haunting of the unclean spirit may be driven away; far hence let the fear of the venomous serpent be cast; and wheresoever it shall be sprinkled, there let the presence of the Holy Spirit be vouchsafed to all of us who shall ask for your mercy. Through your Son Jesus Christ, our Lord, who with you in the unity of the same Holy Spirit lives and reigns, God, world without end. Amen.

The female and male con-celebrants sprinkled the congregation while reciting the following prayers:

Flee, evil spirit of . . .	Come, good spirit of . . .
projection upon the scapegoat	self-acceptance and reconciliation
feminine guilt	self-affirmation and wholeness
fear of the feminine	celebration of the feminine
domination and submission	interdependence and mutuality
the taboos of the body	joy of the body
fear of sexuality	the joy of sexuality
alienation, envy, and jealousy	generosity, participation and community
subterfuge and manipulation	honesty and openness

THE CELEBRATION: "Lady of Birth"

ACT OF THANKSGIVING: "The Vow"—for Anne Hutchinson

sister
your name is not a household word.
maybe you had a 2 line description
in 8th grade history.
more likely you were left out,
as i am when men converse in my presence.
Anne Hutchinson:
"a woman of haughty and fierce carriage."
my shoulders straighten,
you are dead, but not as dead as you
have been, we will avenge you.
you and all the nameless brave spirits,
my mother, my grandmothers,
great grandmothers (Breen Northcott, butcher's wife,
the others forgotten.) who bore me?
generations of denial and misuse

who bore those years of waste? sisters and mothers
it is too late for all of you, waste
& waste again, life after life,
shot to hell. it will take more
than a husband with a nation behind him
to stop me now.

THE REMEMBRANCE

All: Let us remember and give thanks for the women
in our past whose strength gives us strength, whose
struggle for humanity is our struggle, and whose
spirit of independence and dedication is our spirit.
They walk beside us.

For Joan, the Maid of Orleans, and all the sisterhood
of marytrs.

For Martha Corey, Rebecca Nurse, and Mary Esty,
victims of the witchcraft delusion in colonial Massachusetts, killed in 1692.

For Eliza Lucas Pinckney (1722–1793), plantation
manager distinguished for her success in the culti-
vation of indigo in the South.

For Eliza Farnham (1815–1864), prison reformer,
author, lecturer, and early exponent of the superiority of the female sex in her book *Woman and
her Era.*

For Sarah Emma Edmonds (1841–1898), Civil War
soldier who served two years with the Army of the
Potomac in the guise of a man.

For Anna Ella Carroll (1815–1893), military
strategist and the "unofficial member of Lincoln's
Cabinet."

For Margaret Knight (1838–1914), hailed as a
"woman Edison," noted for her numerous inven-
tions concerned with heavy machinery.

For Maud Younger, "Mother of the Eight-Hour Law
and Champion of the Underdog."

SONG: "Union Maid"

For Amelia Bloomer, who published *The Lily,* the first journal ever owned, edited, and controlled by women.

For Belva Lockwood (1830–1917), the first woman to plead before the Supreme Court, and a candidate for the presidency in 1884.

For Hester Stanhope (1776–1839), explorer, who behaved in an "unwomanly" way by wearing men's clothing.

For Aurore Dupin (George Sand), Marianne Evans (George Eliot), and the Bronte sisters (the Bell brothers), who had to use pseudonyms to be published.

For Anna Comstock (1854–1930), naturalist, scientific illustrator and wood engraver, leader in the nature study movement.

For Anne Bradstreet (1616–1672), America's first poet.

For Delia Salter Bacon (1811–1859), author, lecturer, and originator of the theory that Shakespeare's plays were the work of Francis Bacon (no relation).

For Margaret Corbin (1751–1800), Revolutionary War heroine, who fought and was wounded in the battle of Fort Washington.

For Annette Kellerman and Gertrude Ederle, swimmers, and Helen Wills, tennis player, who led to the acceptance of women on a par with men in sports.

SONG: Verses about Billie Jean King

For Phyllis Wheatley (c. 1753–1784), black poet, and America's second female writer in print.

For Katharine Lee Bates (1859–1929), poet, professor of English, and author of "America the Beautiful."

For Frances Benjamin Johnston, Burnice Abbott, and Margaret Bourke-White, forceful, pioneering women photographers.

For Arabella Mansfield (1846–1911), lawyer and college teacher, the first woman admitted to the bar in the U.S.

For Lucinda Foote who in 1783 was found "fully qualified, except in her sex, to be received as a pupil of the freshman class of Yale University."

For Helen White (1853–1944), educator, first American woman to earn a Ph.D. degree.

For Bridget Bishop, hanged as a witch in Salem for unconventionally owning a tavern where she was up late hours, and for refusing to confess.

For Anne Hutchinson, who was banished from Massachusetts for teaching that the Holy Spirit dwells in every believer and that salvation comes by individual intuition of God's grace.

All: We give you thanks for these our sisters.

SONG: "Bread and Roses"

AFFIRMING OUR COMMON HUMANITY

All: Let us affirm our sisters and brothers as we stand together before God.

Men: We believe in God, Creator and Liberator of us all—women and men.

Women: God has freed us from our earthly bonds.

All: In God there is no East nor West,

Men: No slave nor free,

Women: No male nor female.

Men: God's word is liberation.

Women: We are free to realize our dreams.

Men: We need no longer be chained to a cultural image of who we should be.

Women: We as women are strong; there is no "woman's place" we need stay in.

Men: We as men are sometimes weak; we also need to be allowed to cry.

All: We will no longer allow this to be a "man's world."

Men: Dominated by our needs to prove ourselves, to win at all costs,

Women: Self-sacrificing until we no longer have any self,

All: We are all in need of liberation.

Men: We will be tender, caring, loving, supportive.

Women: We will be firm, capable, self-confident.

Men: We affirm you in your struggle for personhood—we will not mock you; instead we will struggle at your side.

Women: We will affirm and share with you those aspects of being female that we all need in these power-hungry times.

All: Praise God! We will be free!

SONG

THE BENEDICTION

The Confession was written by the Reverend Maurine Stephens.
The blessing of salt and water and the combining of the elements were compiled by the Reverend John Scott from traditional sources; Scott also wrote the actual exorcism recited during the sprinkling.
The Remembrance and the final prayer Affirming Our Common Humanity were written by Carol Adams.
Our music was chosen and sung by "Wine, Women, and Song," a local musical group.

8

SISTERHOOD SERVICE ON MOTHER'S DAY

Sydney H. Pendleton

The St. Clement's women's group was formed in 1970 when several of us began to object to the sexism inherent in the language and theology of the church. Our group has usually numbered from six to twelve women including a dancer, a lawyer, a singer, a nurse, an artist-photographer, a producer of radio programs, and several aspiring actresses. We are all daughters and a few of us are also mothers and grandmothers. The women's services we have conducted have all been the main and only service on Sunday morning and have thus included the entire congregation. St. Clement's is a mission church of the Episcopal Diocese of New York which serves the theatrical community, and the church building has been converted into a theater.

For our first service we took the traditional *Book of Common Prayer* liturgy and eliminated the sexist language. For example, we replaced the exclusively male word "Father" with the more inclusive term "Creator." Thus one well-known prayer became the "Our Creator." We also collected sexist quotations from the Bible, male theologians, church fathers, and other men and burned them on the altar. At the prayer of consecration we were forced to rely on the aid of a male priest since women are not yet considered worthy of ordination to the priesthood by the Episcopal church. Some of us felt that the service should have been halted at the point where his participation became necessary —to make clear the position of women in the church. None of our subsequent services had any participation by priests.

Our second service a month later was a celebration of women admired by the members of our group. We read positive quotations about women. These were much harder to find than the negative quotations, there being almost none in the Bible itself. The celebration of the eucharist at the second service was done by Tilda Norberg, an ordained minister in the United Church of Christ.

The Mother's Day service presented here was our third service, for which we had two months to prepare. At our weekly meetings we did consciousness-raising on the subject of motherhood. A member of "It's All Right To Be Woman Theater" held workshops for us so we could learn to express our feelings and to communicate effectively through our actions. Out of these experiences we developed the four skits that would eventually constitute a part of the service. Each skit grew directly out of the life experience of the women who narrated it, and was acted out in pantomime by other members of the group as she was speaking. The work that went into developing the service was tremendously important to all of us as a learning and growing experience, as important as the service itself.

All of us were reading and thinking about ways to express our new insights to the congregation. We developed a litany in which we read verses from all kinds of Mother's Day cards with each verse followed by the traditional litany refrain, "Good Lord, deliver us." The contrast between the versicles and responses not only raised consciousness but proved to be extremely funny.

The music of the chant used during the agape meal was composed by Alice Fix, a member of the group, but the words were a group effort. During the feeding the chant was repeated over and over while different women called out phrases and admonitions they associated with their mothers: "Eat, eat," "Keep your elbows off the table," "Remember the starving children in Europe," "The crusts are the best part," and many more.

Our fourth service four months later was an exploration of the effects of roles and the limitations imposed by them. We decided that priestly functions could be performed by anyone and chose a member of the group by lot to be ordained by the congregation to consecrate the bread and wine for that service. We did this as a prophetic act.

As another part of our exploration of roles we acted out the familiar Mary, Martha, and Jesus story from the Bible (Luke 10:38–41). We improvised our own ending to the story and had Jesus, Mary, and Martha all working in the kitchen together.

A familiar experience for women is the verbal and physical assault we encounter on the streets. To give men a small idea of that experience we asked for volunteers from the congregation to participate in an experiment. The woman stood in a group and, as the men one by one paraded by, the women whistled at them, followed them, commented on their bodies, and even pinched some of them. Afterwards all the participants discussed the experience. The men were made extremely uncomfortable by this experience in spite of the fact that they were in no real danger of assault or rape. The service was filmed by ABC-TV as part of their "Directions" series.

After the fourth service we felt we were being too much identified by other church members as "Those Women" or "The Women's Lib Group." We preferred to be seen as individuals. So, we each wrote and recorded a statement about our own personal experiences in the church. Rena Hansen and Katherine Jones transformed these into a slide-tape which we presented as our sermon in the fifth service. The eucharist followed a pattern similar to the one used in our fourth service. This time, however, members of the congregation were asked to volunteer to serve as celebrant for the service. From among the volunteers one name was selected by lot and that person was ordained by the congregation to break the bread and pour the wine.

All of our services have developed out of our own lives and our consciousness of ourselves as women. The forms we used to express these things were determined by the talents of the group, the context of St. Clement's —which is a theater church—and our sense of the liturgy as theater. All of our services have followed the general outline of the traditional liturgy. They begin with readings, films, skits, and other teaching material followed by feminist forms of the epistle, gospel, and sermon. Then come the offertory and the intercessions followed by the breaking of bread and the drinking of wine.

The liturgy is a form of theater, and putting new material into traditional forms often gives them new power. For instance, when we burned the sexist Bible verses and other quotations on the altar, it was the altar which gave the act its power. Had we burned the same slips of paper on a street corner or anywhere outside the ritual context of the church, the act would have had much less significance. Again, when we used the traditional Litany in conjunction with Mother's Day card verses, it was the interaction of the two forms that brought out the meaning we wanted to share.

I am sure that if we were to do any of these services again we would do it differently. Each of our services has been different from the one before and we have never had the urge to repeat a previous service. We learned a lot about theater, about ourselves, and about the church in the process of doing the services. We found that things from our own lives provided the most powerful medium for sharing our ideas. Theory is dry compared to real life. We found that a discussion period with the congregation is valuable even if time-consuming. After the Mother's Day service, for example, the discussion lasted for nearly two hours—a a clear indication of the fact that our message had indeed reached the congregation, even those who disagreed with us.

Our group recently produced an issue of *The Fourth Quadrant*, St. Clement's quarterly newspaper. Included in it are some of the statements from our services and a history of our group, together with essays, poetry, and visual art by women.

Since then we haven't done anything as a group because our members have simply lost interest in the church. To be continually battling against the church seemed unproductive. As long as the work was creative and beneficial for us, we continued, but eventually it came to seem like a waste of energy. This is not to say that none of us is involved in church activities; indeed, several of us are deeply involved at St. Clement's. We are all engaged in our own spiritual quests, but most of us are now outside the church. We support the efforts of our sisters to be ordained to the priesthood, however, and we all await the day when women will be able to participate fully and equally in all the ministries of the church.

WE'RE CHANGING
WE'RE CHANGING
WE'RE CHANGING
TOGETHER, TOGETHER
WE'RE CHANGING
SANDY BAUER '74

SISTERHOOD SERVICE ON MOTHER'S DAY

INTROIT: "Love Story" from the album *Nilsson Sings Newman* played through twice

LITANY

(A reading of verses from Mother's Day cards, each followed by a sung response:)

Good Lord, deliver us.

WELCOME AND INTRODUCTION TO THE SERVICE

RECORDED MUSIC: Nina Simone singing "For Myself"

READING: "Mother's Day Manifesto"

. . . An important part of the role of mother is the socialization of children into the roles society expects them to fill. These roles, like the role of mother, are often oppressive and damaging. The mother is often blamed by her children for forcing them into these roles, but the mother is as much a victim as the child. She may believe it is better to try to fit into a crippling but socially accepted role than to rebel and be an outcast. She forces her children into these roles for their own good. She is the instrument by which the patriarchal society oppresses children, and her children may in the end feel more resentment than love toward her. . . .

As long as motherhood is not a completely free choice for women, it will continue to produce ambivalent feelings. As long as the care of children devolves completely on women, motherhood will be a trap. As long as women can fulfill themselves only through motherhood and achieve only through their children, children will be oppressed. As long as the growth and potential of women is stunted by the patriarchal system, children will suffer. Only when both women and men can achieve their full potential in a society will children be liberated from the burden of their parents' unfulfilled ambitions.

What will motherhood be in a liberated society? It is difficult to know the answer. But I am convinced that equal rights for all women and men, freedom from stereotyped sex roles, and sharing the responsibility for children are necessary before motherhood can become a truly joyous experience.

READING: "Nice Baby"

SKIT: "Mother as Furniture"

I used to get the feeling that being a mother was like being a piece of furniture. One day when it was getting to me I decided to test my theory. So I washed my hair and I made great big mounds of soap suds on my head. Without washing it off I got dressed and went into the kitchen to get supper.

Jimmy was twelve, Johnny was ten, Mary Katherine was nine, David was eight, and Stephen was five. They were all in and out of the kitchen while I was cooking and they helped set the table. We were three quarters of the way through dinner before David really looked at me and said, "Mother! What have you got on your hair?!"

READING: "Where is it Written?"

MORE SKITS

READING: "Your Children Are Not Your Children"

RECORDED MUSIC: Peggy Lee's "I'm a Woman"

OFFERTORY

ANNOUNCEMENTS

INTERCESSIONS

(Members of the congregation offer their own intercessions)

FEEDING

(Women distribute bread, wine, and cheese to the congregation as we sing our chant:)

Mothers and daughters and sisters, we're changing,
Stronger and braver and freer, we're changing.
We're changing. We're changing. We're changing.
Together, together, we're changing.

FEEDBACK

(We sat on the edge of the stage and asked the congregation to give us their reactions to the service. While we all continued to eat our bread, wine, and cheese, there was a heated discussion which lasted for nearly two hours.)

Rena Hansen welcomed the congregation and introduced the service. Sydney H. Pendleton wrote and read the "Mother's Day Manifesto." Katherine Jones wrote the skit.

9

JEWISH WOMEN'S HAGADA

Aviva Cantor Zuckoff

Several years ago a group of young Jews in New York constituted themselves the Jewish Liberation Project. We came from a variety of backgrounds—Old and New Left, Zionist, religious, Yiddishist—and in time we came to define ourselves as Socialist-Zionists. We became involved in a variety of work within the American Jewish community and on the left. We talked a lot about "alternative politics" and "alternative lifestyles."

A family feeling definitely existed among us in those early years. When Pesach (Passover) came around, we wanted to be able to hold a seder that reflected both our politics and our feeling of community. Thus the Jewish Liberation Seder was born. It was written by three people: Itzhak Epstein, Yaakov (then Jerry) Kirschen, and myself. I wrote the basic draft, drawing on much research and on long discussions with my two collaborators; they helped me cut, refine, and polish it. Kirschen did all the art.

What we wrote was a ceremony that was both Jewish and radical in values and concepts, traditional in ritual, and modern in its pace and language. We tried to tie in the struggle for Jewish liberation today with struggles of our people in the past and to draw on Jewish experience and Jewish sources to speak to what we ourselves were going through.

We began at the obvious point: we cut a lot of what we considered excess verbiage that related to medieval scholastic debates—but added a lot of our own verbiage! We added material on the Holocaust, Israel, and Soviet Jewry. One of the main things we did was to infuse old rituals with new content and meaning. For example, while retaining the four cups of wine that must be drunk at the seder, we attached new meaning to each one, making each stand for a particular struggle against oppression.

A couple of years later, while wandering through a bookstore, I picked up Beverly Jones's and Judith Brown's paper, "Toward a Female Liberation Movement." On reading it I experienced a flash of recognition and identification and promptly became a feminist. More reading and thinking followed. Later I began to do research on the Jewish woman; I lectured on the subject and even taught a course on it at the Jewish Free High School.

About two years after that, as more women were also trying to synthesize their new Jewish consciousness and their feminist consciousness, one woman sent out a circular to all her friends and acquaintances, calling them to a meeting to discuss how we feel and think as Jewish women. Several large meetings followed. A core group of seven women which eventually emerged became my Jewish women's consciousness-raising group. Even though one woman later dropped out and another settled in Israel, the group is still going strong after two years. In our weekly meetings we have tried to understand how our Jewish background has made us what we are, and we are still exploring what it means to be a Jewish woman.

After a year, having become close and loving friends, we decided that we wanted to hold a Jewish Women's Seder. We felt that we were a family and that we could

use this most Jewish of ceremonies to bring us and
other Jewish women closer to each other and to our
history and values. What follows are excerpts from the
seder I put together for this occasion. In true Pesach
spirit, the seder was written in haste (like the matzo
baked by the Jews escaping Egypt).

Because of the rush, I did not write the hagada from
scratch. I took the Jewish Liberation Hagada, used it as
a basic framework, cut some material and then added
feminist material. My first shock came in rereading the
Jewish Liberation Hagada. First, I was bothered by the
obvious things: the four sons, the "he" all over the
place not followed by "and she." But even more dis-
turbing—especially since I was the main author of the
hagada—was the almost complete absence of women,
our invisibility. Except for one poem there was very
little to indicate that Jewish women had been active
participants in Jewish life and struggles.

So I rewrote the seder, first taking care of the minor
changes: making God "ruler of the universe" instead of
"king," adding the names of Jacob's wives to the exodus narrative, and changing "four sons" to "four
daughters." The major change was to utilize the four
cups ritual and to dedicate each cup of wine to the
struggle of Jewish women in a particular period. The
hagada's aim was to provide connecting links between
Jewish women of the past and us here in the present. A
great deal of material came from Jewish legends and
historical sources, some only recently discovered. Although the seder proved enjoyable to us and our friends,
I still feel quite dissatisfied with it and regard it in no
way as complete.

The first and most obvious problem is the fact that
this seder is based on another seder and is therefore not
really "original." Although beautiful in many respects,
it represents an almost verbatim takeover of its "prede-

cessor's" account of the exodus. Then too, changing
"four sons" to "four daughters" while leaving the rest
of the segment (written by Itzhak Epstein) largely intact
makes that excerpt less relevant than it might be if it
were completely rewritten.

However, there is a more fundamental problem involved in writing a seder for Jewish women and that is
the tension between the very nature of the seder and
the needs of the participants. I think this tension cannot be fully resolved, and whoever writes such a seder
should be aware of it.

On the one hand, the seder is a *Jewish* celebration. It
marks a *specific*—national—liberation from a *specific*
—national—oppression. The Jewish woman, however,
cannot celebrate this liberation with a whole heart
because she knows that *her* oppression continues. This
fact might lead us to want to incorporate into the
hagada a whole lot of material on the oppression of
women in Jewish life, and indeed my first draft did
just that. But that would bring us into conflict with
the essential nature of the seder, which is joyous and
emphasizes those things that unite Jews rather than
divide them (for example, at a seder we do not stress
the class struggle).

Thus the women's seder is in danger of becoming
irrelevant to the needs of its participants. The only
solution I could see was to draw on Jewish history, ex-
tracting material about the participation of Jewish
women in the struggles for Jewish liberation (which is
the theme of the seder). Emphasizing our participation
in Jewish struggles, however, creates two problems: (1)
It makes it seem as if the hagada is our "entrance card"
to Jewish society, as if through it we were saying,
"Look, we're *real Jews* after all." (2) It makes it seem
as if Jewish women have never had any problem at all
in Jewish society, as if they have always been allowed

to participate as equals, and, this, of course, is untrue. So the question remains: how to deal with the oppression of the Jewish woman *within the context of the seder as a ceremony marking Jewish national liberation*. As yet I have no answer to this question; perhaps women can find the solution together.

My final reservation about the Jewish Women's Hagada is even more basic. As much as I loved a seder with my sisters, what gnawed at me was my memory of the seders I had at home, in my parents' house, seders of men and women of several generations, with children running underfoot and spilling the wine. The seder has always been a family celebration and, for me, a seder just for women seems incomplete.

What I would like to see—and for me it has not yet crystallized—is a seder that focuses on the oppression of Jews and on Jewish liberation *from a Jewish feminist viewpoint*. Such a hagada would deal honestly with the oppression of women while keeping the main focus on Jewish liberation. It would be a seder for families of all kinds, whether by blood or by choice. In such a seder, women would be as "visible" as men, but neither men nor women would be the entire focus of the seder. This is the kind of seder I would like to take my children to—if and when I ever have children. I would also, of course, invite my dear friend Nadia Borochov Ovsey who celebrated her ninetieth birthday in October of 1973, the woman of valor to whom I dedicated this hagada.

JEWISH WOMEN'S HAGADA

Chaverot, shalom.

We have gathered here tonight to celebrate Pesach, the festival of the liberation of the Jewish people. Pesach is the night when all the families of Israel gather to celebrate and to strengthen their ties—to each other and to all Jews. We too are a family, a growing family. We too have ties we hope to strengthen. For while we are not related by blood, we are related by something perhaps even stronger: sisterhood.

Then follows the blessing on the wine, the dipping of the greens in salt water, the breaking of the middle matza, the Four Questions, and the core of the seder—the telling of the story of the Jews' struggle for liberation from slavery in Egypt. As the first cup of wine—dedicated to the first uprising of the Jews against oppression and the first liberation—is lifted, the following blessing is said:

As we hold this cup of wine, we remember our sisters in the land of Egypt who fearlessly stood up to the Pharaoh.

Our legends tell us that Pharaoh, in the time-honored pattern of oppressors, tried to get Jews to collaborate in murdering their own people. He summoned the top two Jewish midwives, Shifra and Pu'ah—some legends say one of them was Yocheved, who was also Moshe's mother—and commanded them to kill newborn Jewish males at birth and to report the birth of Jewish females so that they could be raised to become prostitutes. Pharaoh tried at first to win over the midwives by making sexual advances to them. When they repulsed these, he threatened them with death by fire. The midwives did not carry out Pharaoh's command. Instead of murdering the male infants, they took special care of them. If a mother was poor, they went around to the other women, collecting food for her and her child. When Pharaoh asked the midwives to account for all the living children, they made up the excuse that Jewish women gave birth so fast that they did not summon midwives in time.

Like our Jewish sisters through the ages, those in Egypt

were strong and courageous in the face of oppression. Our sages recognized this when they said: "The Jews were liberated from Egypt because of the righteousness of the women."

The parable of the four sons is here retold as "The Four Daughters," in language reflecting our struggle to find ourselves as Jewish women. The nature of oppression is also defined and the Holocaust described in "Go and Learn":

Go and learn how the enemies of the Jews have tried so many times and in so many places to destroy us. We survived because of our spiritual resistance and our inner strength. Throughout the ages Jewish women have provided this strength, courage, and loyalty. During very desperate times, Jewish women were allowed to openly show their strength. Yocheved, Miriam, Deborah, Yael, Judith, Esther, who was called a "redeemer"—how few are the names of the heroic Jewish women which have come down to us! How many more were there whose names we will never know?

We speak of rebellion as the only way to overthrow oppression. The Ten Plagues are mentioned one by one. Then we raise and dedicate the second cup of wine to the ghetto fighters.

We drink this second of four cups of wine to honor the glorious memory of the Jewish fighters in the ghettos, concentration camps, and forests of Nazi Europe. They fought and died with honor and avenged the murder of our people. Their courage and hope in the face of unutterable brutality and despair inspires us.

As we hold this cup of wine, we remember our glorious and brave sisters who fought so courageously against the Nazi monsters. We remember Hannah Senesch and Haviva Reik, who parachuted behind enemy lines in Hungary and Slovakia to organize

resistance and rescue Jews. We remember Vladka
Meed, and Chaika and Frumka Plotnitski, who
served as couriers and smuggled arms for the ghetto
fighters. We remember Rosa Robota who organized
the smuggling of dynamite to blow up a crematorium
in Auschwitz. Chaika Grossman, Gusta Drenger,
Zivia Lubetken, Gisi Fleischman, Tosia Altman,
Zofia Yamaika, Niuta Teitelboim—these are but a
few of the names we know. Their willingness to sacrifice their lives for their people shines through the
words of Hanna Senesch, written shortly before her
execution (Nov. 7, 1944):

> Blessed is the match that is consumed
>   in kindling the flame
> Blessed is the flame that burns
>   in the secret fastness of the heart
> Blessed is the heart strong enough to
>   stop beating in dignity
> Blessed is the match that is consumed
>   in kindling the flame.

We sing the traditional Dayeynu, *eat matza and the bitter herbs
and discuss their symbolism, and then talk of liberation and
the importance of the Jewish homeland.*

In every century Jews longed to return to Zion. In our
own day, many Soviet Jews are struggling for their
right to settle in Israel. Ruth Alexandrovitch, Raiza
Palatnik, and Sylva Zalmanson were imprisoned for
their part in this struggle. Sylva is still held in the
notorious Potma labor camp, serving a ten-year
sentence for being part of a group charged with trying to hijack a plane to leave the country.

When the Prophet Jeremiah watched the Jews being
led away into Babylonian captivity, he saw a vision
of our Matriarch, Rachel, a symbol of this tragedy
and of the yearning to return to Eretz Yisrael:

A voice is heard on high
A keening, mournful wail.
Rachel is crying for her children
Refusing to be consoled
For their loss.

The Lord says:
Hold back the cries in your throat
And the tears in your eyes
For there is a future of hope for you:
Your children shall return
To their own land. (*Jer. 31:15–18*)

The third cup of wine is blessed.

We drink the third cup of wine to honor the Jews of
   our own time who fought and died to establish Israel.
As we lift this cup of wine, we also bring to mind our
   many sisters in Israel who started the "first wave" of
   feminism there. We remember the haluzot, the
   women pioneers who won their struggle to work in the
   fields and as laborers in the cities—as equals in the
   upbuilding of Israel.
We remember our sisters Manya Schochat, Sarah
   Malchin, Yael Gordon, Techia Lieberson, Hannah
   Meisel, and so many others, who set up women's
   collectives and women's agricultural training farms
   and organized the working women's movement in
   Eretz Yisrael. We remember two of these organizers,
   Sarah Chisick and Dvora Drachler, who fell in the
   defense of Tel-Hai with Yosef Trumpeldor. We remember our many sisters who fought in the under-
   ground and in the army during the War of Independence.
In Passover of 1911, the first meeting of working
   women in Eretz Yisrael was held. "The girls who had
   the opportunity to work in the fields were few and

far between and even within the pioneering, revolutionary labor movement in the Land of Israel,
women were relegated to their traditional tasks—
housekeeping and particularly kitchen work. . . .
The men tended to belittle the women's problems
and accused the girls of being oversensitive. . . .

"The girls wanted very much to discuss ways of changing and improving the situation. A meeting of their
own, they felt, was absolutely necessary, for it had become clear that women would not raise their voices at
general conferences and that the male delegates would
not put the special problems of women workers on the
agenda.

"The first meeting of the working women took place in
Kvutzat Kinneret. There were 17 participants. . . .
The proceedings went on behind closed doors; no
men were allowed to attend. The girls were too un-
accustomed to public speaking, particularly in
Hebrew, to tolerate onlookers; and, in addition, they
suspected the men of being curious rather than truly
concerned. Actually some men tried to listen from
behind the doors and windows to hear 'them' talk.
Emotional outpouring rather than systematic analysis
of problems characterized the meeting." From this
meeting the Working Women's Movement was born.

*We talk of what Jewish identity means and how assimilation is
self-oppression. We bless and then drink the fourth and last
cup of wine.*

We drink this fourth and last cup of wine on this seder
night to honor all our Jewish sisters who are struggling to find new and beautiful ways to say "I am a
Jew."

We honor all our sisters in the small but growing Jewish women's movement, some of whom are just meeting each other today; and all our sisters everywhere—

Orthodox, secular, Conservative, Zionist, Reconstruc-
tionist, Bundist, Reform, radical, gay, young, old,
middle-aged; our mothers and our grandmothers
whom we have so long misunderstood and fought;
our daughters; and all our sisters who are now coming together to say: We are Jewish women and we
are proud.

Assimilation is the opposite of Jewish pride and Jewish
consciousness. It is a suicide trip, and a trap for all
the Jewish people. It is a trap that Jewish men fell
into when they came to this country and thought
wealth and power could also be theirs, as white
males, if they gave up their Jewishness. Too many
were in a great hurry to jettison everything Jewish as
excess baggage that would hinder their upward
mobility. Having done so, they benefitted from all
the "advantages" of assimilation. But they did not
realize that the price was too high. Nor did they see
that this assimilation was oppressive to them.

We Jewish women could see this more clearly because,
as women, we had nothing much to gain by assimilat-
ing; no power was open to us anyway. But our men
wanted assimilated wives and daughters. They have
tried to make us over, to look and behave like the
non-Jewish women in the economic bracket they
aspire to. They have tried to make us change our hair
and our noses, and to stop yelling, to be genteel and
submissive. They have tried to program us to teach
our children to assimilate, too. Many of us have almost destroyed ourselves trying to be what we are not.
We have tried to change ourselves, to mutilate our
noses and to straighten our hair, to be "good wives"
and above all, "good mothers." We have done this and
have been ridiculed as "Jewish princesses" and "Jewish mothers."

We have come to realize how stupid, empty, mean-

ingless, and destructive the assimilationist trip is.
Many of our Jewish brothers are still into assimila-
tionism—although some are trying to climb out of
it—and the organized Jewish community certainly
is. But *we* have begun to cast off the assimilationist
dream that has turned into a nightmare. We are
becoming ourselves. It is very possible that, in liberating ourselves from the need to be like everybody
else, from the fear of being conspicuously Jewish,
and in moving toward building Jewish lifestyles, re-
discovering our history and our traditions, our heritage and our values, and building on them and from
them, we shall at one and the same time be instru-
mental in the struggle to liberate the Jewish people
as well. That too is our goal.

*Now we speak of what we've been waiting for—the food! We eat,
sing, eat the* afikoman, *say Grace After Meals, and sing the
traditional* Chad Gadya—*"One Goatling." After singing "Next
Year in Jerusalem," we conclude*:

We have talked on this Pesach night about our liberation from oppression and thus we conclude the formal part of the seder. Just as we have been privileged
to hold this seder with our sisters so may we be privileged to join with them in struggling for our liberation as Jewish women. May we carry out our self-
liberation soon, joyously returning to our heritage
and our homeland and our people—to be redeemed
and to participate in the redemption of the Jewish
people.

Next Year in Jerusalem!

NOTES

Page

4 "God of the Matriarchs": The liturgy was previously published in *Liturgy*, the membership journal of the Liturgical Conference, in March, 1973. Reprinted here with the permission of the Liturgical Conference.

4 "O God, Thou Art the Father": See *Pilgrim Hymnal* (Boston: Pilgrim Press, 1962), p. 248.

6 "Lo, How a Rose E'er Blooming": See *Pilgrim Hymnal,* p. 131.

16 "Sojourner Truth": See Leslie Tanner, ed., *Voices from Women's Liberation* (New York: Signet, 1971), p. 73.

17 "Have a Nice Day": See Norman Habel, *Hi! Have a Nice Day* (Philadelphia: Fortress, 1972), p. 15.

18 "Love One Another": See *Hymnal for Young Christians* (Chicago: F.E.L. Church Publications, 1968), p. 23.

31 "It's a Long Road to Freedom": See Medical Mission Sisters, *Joy is Like the Rain* (New York: Avant Garde Records).

33 "Sojourner Truth": See Eleanor Flexner, *Century of Struggle* (New York: Atheneum, 1970), pp. 90-91.

33 "Fiat": An original poem by Joan Krofta.

33 "St. Catherine of Siena": See her diary as quoted in Sidney Callahan, *The Illusion of Eve* (New York: Sheed and Ward, 1965), p. 86.

34 "Joy is Like the Rain": See *Joy is Like the Rain.*

34 "Spirit of God": See *Joy is Like the Rain.*

46 "Daughters of God": Sung to tune of "Sons of God," in *Hymnal for Young Christians,* p. 40.

46 "One in the Spirit": See *Hymnal for Young Christians,* p. 74.

51 "Applesource: The Coming of Lilith": See *The Women's Pulpit* (October-December, 1972), p. 7.

54 "Free to be You and Me": See Marlo Thomas and Friends, *Free to be You and Me* (New York: Columbia Records).

54 "Lady of Birth": By Ruth Duck, copyright © 1973 by Ruth Duck, reprinted with the permission of the author.

56 "The Trial": Information about the play, not reprinted here, may be obtained from PTFWR, Box 24003, Phila., Pa. 19139.

58 "Notable American Women": See Edward T. James and Janet W. James, *Notable American Women,* 3 vols. (Boston, Harvard University, 1971).

58 "Generations of Denial": See Kathryn Taylor, ed., *Generations of Denial* (New York: Times Change Press, 1971).

58 "Century of Struggle": See Eleanor Flexner, *Century of Struggle* (New York: Atheneum, 1968).

58 "The Liberated Woman's Songbook": See Jerry Silverman, *The Liberated Woman's Songbook* (New York: Macmillan, 1971).

58 "Ruth Duck": See "Lady of Birth" on p. 54 of this book.

63 "The Vow": A poem by Alta. See Kathryn Taylor, ed., *Generations of Denial* (New York: Times Change Press, 1971). Copyright © 1971 by Times Change Press, 62 W. 14 St., New York, New York 10011. Reprinted with the permission of the publisher.

64 "Union Maid": See *The Liberated Woman's Songbook*, p. 78.

66 "Bread and Roses": See *ibid.*, p. 60.

70 "Filmed Service": See "Feminism and the Church," which can be rented from the BCF-TV Film Library, 475 Riverside Drive, New York, New York 10027.

71 "Slide-tape": The slide tape, slightly edited, and a film strip version of it are available through "Radio Free People," 133 Mercer Street, New York, New York 10012.

72 *"Fourth Quadrant"*: Copies of the Spring, 1973, issue are available for 35¢ from St. Clement's Church, 423 West 46 Street, New York, New York 10036.

74 "Love Story": See "Nilsson Sings Newman" (New York: RCA Records).

74 "For Myself": See Nina Simone, *Let It All Out* (New York: Philips Records).

74 "Manifesto": "Mother's Day Manifesto" by Sydney H. Pendleton. Copyright © 1971 by Sydney H. Pendleton. Reprinted with the permission of the author.

75 "Nice Baby": See Judith Viorst, *It's Hard to be Hip Over Thirty and Other Tragedies of Married Life* (New York: Norton, 1968), p. 21.

75 "Where Is It Written?": See *ibid.*, p. 43.

75 "Your children are not your children": See Kahlil Gibran, *The Prophet* (New York: Alfred A. Knopf, 1969), p. 17.

75 "I'm a Woman": See Peggy Lee, *Is That All There Is?* (New York: Capital Records).

81 "Hagada": The *Jewish Women's Hagada*, here abbreviated, is published by the Jewish Liberation Project, 150 Fifth Avenue, New York, New York 10011. Copyright © 1973 by the Jewish Liberation Project. Reprinted by permission.

82 "Pharoah": See Louis Ginzburg, *Legends of the Jews*, 3 vols. (Philadelphia: Jewish Publication Society of America, 1956).

83 "Righteousness of the women": See the Babylonian Talmud, Sota 11 b.

83 "Hanna Senesch": A translation from the Hebrew by Aviva Cantor Zuckoff.

85 "Passover of 1911": See Ada Maimon, *Women Build a Land* (New York: Herzl, 1962), p. 28. Copyright © 1962 by the Theodor Herzl Foundation. Reprinted by permission.